MW01145809

Sunshine and Smiles

Life Story, Flash Lights, Sayings, and Sermons

by

Rev. Bud Robinson

First Fruits Press
Wilmore, Kentucky
2015

Sunshine and Smiles: Life Story, Flash Lights, Sayings, and Sermons
by Bud Robinson

Published by First Fruits Press, © 2015
Previously published by the Christian Witness Company, ©1903

ISBN: 9781621711933 (print), 9781621711926 (digital)

Digital version at
http://place.asburyseminary.edu/firstfruitsheritagematerial/93/

Robinson, Bud, 1860-1942.
    Sunshine and smiles : life story, flash lights, sayings and
    sermons / by Bud Robinson.
    [Second edition].
    191 pages : portrait ; 21 cm.
    Wilmore, KY : First Fruits Press, ©2015.
    Reprint. Previously published: Chicago, IL : Christian Witness
    Company, ©1903.
    ISBN: 9781621711933 (pbk.)
    1. Robinson, Bud, 1860-1942. 2. Holiness Churches – United
    States. 3. Evangelists – United States – Biography. 4. Holiness –
    Sermons. 5. Evangelistic sermons. I. Title.
BX7990.H6 R7 2015   234.8

Cover design by Wesley Wilcox

First Fruits Press
The Academic Open Press of Asbury Theological Seminary
204 N. Lexington Ave., Wilmore, KY 40390
859-858-2236
first.fruits@asburyseminary.edu
asbury.to/firstfruits

REV. BUD ROBINSON

SUNSHINE AND SMILES

LIFE STORY
FLASH LIGHTS
SAYINGS AND SERMONS

BY

BUD ROBINSON

THE CHRISTIAN WITNESS COMPANY
CHICAGO AND BOSTON
1904

ROBT. O. LAW CO., PRINTERS AND BINDERS, CHICAGO.

DEDICATION.

I lovingly dedicate this book to the whole human family, to whom I am indebted for every idea expressed in it, for when I came into this world I knew nothing at all, not even the way to my mouth.

Yours for the glory of God and the good of Humanity.

BUD ROBINSON.

PUBLISHERS' NOTE TO
SECOND EDITION

The favor with which the first edition of "Sunshine and Smiles" has met suggests the advisability of increasing the usefulness of this second edition by revising and improving it. Much matter has been added to the story of this wonderful life. To bring out the contrast between sin and grace even more clearly a number of half-tone illustrations are given showing how a poor ignorant mountain boy can, by the mighty power of God, be transformed into a flaming torch of Divine light and power, bringing the news of salvation to thousands of precious souls and leading them from the thraldom of sin into perfect liberty in Christ. That this unpretentious little volume may, with its author—a miracle of grace—be used of God in bringing multitudes to the Fountain that cleanseth from all sin, and in establishing many in the faith of an uttermost salvation, is the earnest and sincere prayer of

THE PUBLISHERS.

CONTENTS.

LIFE STORY.

FLASH LIGHTS.

SAYINGS AND SERMONS.

ILLUSTRATIONS

LIFE STORY.

CHAPTER I.

EARLIEST RECOLLECTIONS.

I moved to America on January 27th, 1860. I met a cold reception, of course, as the snow was something like knee deep and I was very thinly clad, just having the suit that nature provided for me. I settled in White county, Tennessee. My first employment was to work for my living, and my mother said I was a good rustler, but I used up my income as fast as I got it.

If it were not that God was to have the glory, I'd never want to tell of the poverty or ignorance or hardships I've waded through. I expect when I've been in heaven a week, I'll forget I ever went barefooted in this country. Right where the devil had his den there shall be a palace of flowers. The redeemed shall walk on the highway of holiness.

Out of the 1,189 chapters in the Bible, the 35th chapter of Isaiah comes nearer being my experience than any I can find. I have read them all on my knees, and on my feet, sitting down and standing up and lying down; I have read them by sunshine and by moonshine and by electricity and by lamp light. I have never been so

poor that I did not have sunshine, and moonshine a part
of the time, but I have been too poor to buy kerosene
oil and I had to study by moonshine when I studied by
night. I have studied the Bible by moonshine, lying
in the yard, face downward. I would rather do that
than not to read it at all. There is so much in it that
if a man has not time to read it by sunshine, and is too
poor to buy oil, he ought to thank God for moonshine,
and get out into the yard and read it. The man who
wants to go to heaven has the way open to go, and men
and devils can't hold him. Glory to God!

Now I see the real leadings of God all along the line.
There were a number of years that he seemed to be hid
from me, but I did want to do right at all times, but I
have realized the last few years that God is real near.
When I got the consent of my mind to let Him save
me, He was there to save me.

I was born in the mountains of Tennessee in the very
lowest depths of poverty in an old log cabin without any
chimney to it, only a mud chimney about half way to
the top, a dirt floor and one room in the house and but
little furniture; no cook stove, no sewing machine in it,
nothing of the kind; no bookcase nor wardrobe. No
carpets of any kind, but simply the face of the earth,
but that is not a bad place to be born, especially if a
fellow does not intend to do anything after he is born.

READING THE SCRIPTURES BY MOONLIGHT.

There is where I was born in that log cabin. Such a thing as schools and churches were unknown there on the mountains where I was born.

It matters little how my life starts, if it ends with a chariot and some angels. I started out in poverty, and my father was unfortunately in the whisky business. When a man gives his time to ruining men, it don't take long to go to the bottom. I was hungry and cold, and slept on a sheepskin with a dog often. I didn't know there was such a thing as a church or school house in the world. I've had people to make fun of me all my life, but why didn't you come and help me?

My baby buggy was not a carriage but a hollow log, about four feet long, split open, making a nice little trough, with an old quilt in it and a pillow. I spent several months as happy as a lark. My mother sat by me and carded wool and cotton rolls to spin her thread. As mother sat there by the old log fire and sung the sweetest old songs in the world, I had nothing to do but lie there in the little cradle—as it was called—and listen to mother sing, play with my hands, suck my thumb and go to sleep. As mother carded she rocked the cradle with her foot, looked down into the trough and talked all kinds of baby talk to me and said many a time that Little Buddie was sure to make his mark in the world.

Well, my friends, I want to stop long enough to tell

you I made the mark; it was a long, black, crooked one. The hope of the race is the confidence a mother puts in her children. Every true mother can see something in her boy that other people can't see. The reason we can't see something in them is because they are not our boys. The reason she does is because he is her boy. She looks beyond his misfortunes and sees in him great possibilities and in her heart full of love she knows that success is sure to come—with the smile of hope on her face she sees fortune just ahead.

By this time you are anxious to know whether or not the baby boy ever got out of the hollow log. Of course he did; don't you know that you can't keep a boy forever in a hollow log? I told you at the start that the log was only four feet long. I soon outgrew it and mother had to put breeches on me and turn me loose with the other children. About this time in life recollection came into use; the first thing I remember was the soldiers going by with blue coats on, the next thing was my mother coming through the cornfield shouting. She was coming from the spring that was over at the back of the little cornfield—it was one of those beautiful springs flowing out from under the great mountain, as clear as crystal and so cold it would make your teeth ache, just running over the white sand and gravel, sunperch, red bass and speckled trout playing under the rocks that stuck out over the branch all covered with ferns and mountain moss. Surely that was one of the prettiest places in the world, and while mother was over there getting water, the same Christ that met the woman at the well, met mother, and while she was filling her bucket with water, the Lord filled her soul with grace, and she came through the field with her bucket in one hand, waving the other over her head, praising the Lord. Occasionally she would set the bucket down and go to clapping her hands and shouting in the old style. It was Glory! Glory!! Hallelujah, Bless God forever! We children ran out and climbed up on the yard fence, where we could just see mother's head as she jumped up and down in the corn rows. She came on to the house bareheaded, and spilt nearly all the water and lost her bonnet, but she had a shine on her face I never will forget.

I was at that time about four years old, and mother's shouting put me under such deep conviction I had no rest from the sense of guilt and condemnation. I wanted religion worse than anything in the world. I well remember going down into the apple orchard, getting down on my knees under the old horse-apple tree to pray. I don't know why I didn't get religion unless it was because of the wickedness of my father. He was very profane and would come in the house and swear bitterly. This would excite me very much and for the time being I would forget the struggles of my poor little heart.

The earliest recollections of my father are when he was in a difficulty and was trying to kill one of his neighbors. He had his gun in his hand and a man was holding him to hinder him from carrying out his intentions.

There are pictures that remain in the child's memory like burrs in a sheep's wool; the next one that took fast hold of mine was a difficulty between mother and a Yankee soldier. My father had been run off from home and all the horses taken but one old sorrel mare with a blaze face and one eye out, "Old Gin" we called her. Mother and we children hauled wood on the sled with "Old Gin." One morning mother went out to feed her and the Yankee soldier told her to feed that mare well, for he expected to ride her that day. Of course the war opened right there. Mother told him never in this world would he ride "Old Gin." She fed the mare and we children stayed out in the yard to see whether or not the Yankee was coming to get her. About the time "Old Gin" finished up her breakfast the Yankee was at the barn door with mother and us children, and the circus opened up. He opened the barn door and went in to put the bridle on the mare and mother took it off. He began to curse and mother was shaking her fist in his face, calling him all sorts of hard names. He put the bridle on again and mother pulled it off. By this time he was pretty hot, and jerked an old pistol out of his belt and we children began to scream as loud as we could and hold to mother's dress. He swung the revolver over his head, and cursed. By this time mother was at white heat and hit him right over the head and face with the bridle just as hard as she could put it on him. Then the regular fight took place; they clinched and scuffled over the barn for some little time while we children were almost having spells. Finally he shoved mother up against the barn door and hurt her side, and before she could regain her strength and renew the battle he had put the bridle on "Old Gin," led her out of the barn and was riding away. Mother stood in the barn door, shaking her fist after him and saying in a loud voice: "You'd better get a good ride today, because this is the last day you will ever ride 'Old Gin,' for if God spares my life I will have old Pleas Parr and the Texas guerrillas on your track before night." He laughed at her and rode on. Of course mother was only threatening him, as she had no idea that the guerrillas were anywhere in the country.

The little squad of Yankee soldiers—about seventy-five in number—went on up the road about twelve miles from our house on the little Calf Killer river, stopping at a house where there was a sick woman and a lot of old women had gathered in to wait on her. The soldiers began to exchange horses with the women without their consent and put some of them to cooking dinner for them. While they were eating, swapping horses and mistreating the old women, old Pleas Parr and his band of Texas guerrillas came across the mountains from East Tennessee, ran upon them and surely made it hot for the boys. Pleas Parr and his men fought under the black flag. They never gave nor took prisoners, and they had six shooters belted on them from their necks to their knees. I suppose the Texas guerrillas, as they were called, were among the worst men in the world. At their appearance the blue coats leaped into their saddles and went down the road at full speed, the guerrillas after them. Every few hundred yards they would shoot one off his horse and some one of the band would get down and cut off his head. By the time they had reached our place they had killed most all the soldiers. They went by at full speed with their horses covered with foam and dust, their mouths open and tongues out, with the sound of revolvers every minute, men hollering and pleading for their lives. What a sad day. God forbid that we should ever see another like it. As they came near our house "Old Gin" left

BUD ROBINSON'S MOTHER
(1902)

the main road, turned round the corner of the field and coming to a deep gully tried to jump it, but failed and went head foremost into the gully right on top of the soldier that had whipped mother that morning. The guerrillas, supposing they had killed both horse and rider, went on after the rest. After they had all passed by the soldier got out of the gully, ran through the field and made his escape. Mother and we children went down and got "Old Gin," led her to the house, bound up her limbs, carried her water and worked with her for a week before she was sufficiently recovered from her ride to assume her duties.

That soldier may have forgotten some things in his life but there is one day's work that will never be erased from his memory. The day he whipped mother, took "Old Gin" and met the Texas crowd, will remain fresh in his memory until he meets his black box, and all the preachers in the world will never be able to convince that fellow that mother was not to blame for the whole affair. I think I can just see that poor man now out in the mountains that night, under a rock raking up a few leaves to make him a bed, going to sleep about midnight, cursing rebels, and in his dreams seeing women and children, blazed face horses, bridles, pistols, Texas guerrillas, deep gullies and such like.

About this time in my life my mother had a strange

dream about me.   She dreamed she had to offer
me as a sacrifice on the altar just as Abraham   offered   Isaac,   and   that   I   was to be
offered for the whole family, and without it
the family would be lost.   In her dream she built the
altar, bound me, laid me on the altar and the Lord told
her to take my life.   She screamed and plead with the
Lord to spare me, awoke and rejoiced to find it only a
dream, went back to sleep and dreamed the same thing
again, and in the last dream she saw that all the suffering that could be put on me didn't seem to take my life
and that mine was to be a life of suffering and sacrifice
and through my suffering the rest of the family was to
be brought to Christ.   This dream made a great impression on my mind; it renewed conviction and created
such a desire in my heart for religion that I never could
wear it off, and with all the fun—as I called it—in
my life I was never easy until the night I was converted
—in my 21st year.   No one could persuade mother her
dream has not been fulfilled in her Buddie's life.   I
will leave it for others who knew me to judge.

CHAPTER II.

In my fifth year the war was over, our father had come home, sold out his land and bought wagons and horses and we prepared to move to Mississippi. We left the mountains of Tennessee in the fall of 1865 and just before Christmas we landed in Tipper county, Mississippi, settled on the little Tallahassie river, where there were more fish and mud turtles, mosquitoes and water moccasins than any place in America. We stayed in Mississippi four years. The first year was one of misfortune and hardship; our horses all died with blind staggers. My father rented a farm from a man who was to furnish us teams. When the crop was planted the man went back on his contract and he and my father had trouble—he was a very mean man and my father was just as mean as he. After my father lost his crop he rented a still from a man and went to making whisky. He did not work at that long until he and the man who owned the still had trouble, fought and came near killing each other. That was another dark day.

By the time we were through with the whisky business all of our property was gone but one wagon and

14808

two milk cows, and now he traded the cows for a little yoke of steers and moved out into the pinery and went to burning tar for a living, which was a very hard life. There are not many boys nowadays that ever saw a tar kiln. First you go through the woods and gather up the pine knots and put them in piles, then go back over the ground with your wagon and haul your knots to the kiln, then split up your knots and build a tar kiln, and burn and get the tar out. I will not go into detail and try to explain the process of burning the kiln, but it was a very hard job and the dirtiest work in the world. We were in the tar business three years. We generally built about three kilns a year and would run from five to six hundred gallons out of a kiln and sell it for about 40 cents per gallon. It was used all over the country for axle grease, every wagon having a tar gourd hanging on the coupling pole. We spent the wet weather and Sundays, hunting and fishing. The woods were full of deer and turkeys. You could hear the turkeys gobbling every morning and often you would see a deer run across the road. We caught fish and swamp rabbits, killed snakes until we quit numbering, ate muscadines, fought mosquitoes and ticks, and I reckon had the hardest and biggest chills in Mississippi. We children passed off the time at night sitting by a big fire built of pine knots, telling riddles and chewing pine wax.

At the end of our four years' struggle we reached the fall of '69 and with a few household goods on the old wagon, the little steers hitched to it, a big tar gourd full of tar swung in on the coupling pole, mother on the wagon with the baby on her lap and seven other children either on the wagon or afoot playing along the road, we now bid the old Tallahassie and the swamps of the Mississippi a hearty farewell. We are now on the road for the mountains of old Tennessee again. My father walks ahead of the wagon with a musket on his shoulder, my oldest brother drives the little steers. We children ride time about, three or four on the wagon, the others walking up the sandy road playing in the sand or stopping under the chestnut trees and picking up chestnuts, or climbing the fence and getting into some fellow's orchard. We would strike up camps on some little creek or at some spring, a little before sundown, unyoke and feed "Nig" and "Jerry" (the little oxen), build a big chunk fire, then we boys were up the creek with our dog in a few minutes to see if we couldn't start a rabbit. It was "seek, seek, there he goes," and away Dixie would go after him. In a few moments he runs him into a hollow tree or log. We chop him out so quick it would make your head swim. We are now back with the rabbit, dressing him for supper. Mother brings the skillet and lid out of the wagon, puts them on the fire, and while they are heating she brings out the corn meal, bread tray and sifter. Now she puts the skillet on coals of fire and proceeds to make up her bread. She sifts the meal in the big tray and makes up the dough with her hands, puts three nice pones in the skillet, puts on the lid, putting coals on that. She then gets the frying pan out of the wagon and goes to frying the rabbit.

Now, reader, just think of it! Old fashioned corn bread cooked in a skillet and fried rabbit for supper! My, my, I can just smell that rabbit and taste that corn bread until now. That was thirty-four years ago. It seems to be only yesterday. I can almost see the little creek and the old water elm standing by the ford, Dixie lying under the wagon, the little oxen having eaten their supper, lying down to rest. Now mother brings out an old quilt or two, makes a big pallet by the fire. A dozen or more little red feet are turned to the chunk fire and we are off to the land of dreams.

About the break of day we hear father calling "Boys! boys!! It is time to get up, make a fire, and feed the steers." So in a few minutes we are up throwing the chunks together and shucking corn for Nig and Jerry. While mother is getting breakfast we cut a pole about fifteen feet long and a little short fork about three feet long to grease the wagon with. We run one end of the long pole under the wagon and three or four of us boys get under the other end and raise the wagon and put the little fork under to hold it up. We now get the wagon hammer and drive out the lynch pin, take off the wheel and get the tar gourd off of the coupling pole, and with a little paddle we put the tar on the axle and a few paddles full into the wheel to make it run light during the day, and by night you could hear it squeak a quarter of a mile. The next morning we would have to tar up again. We kept this up every morning for three weeks until we reached the Tennessee mountains. I remember as we went through Alabama, in one of the little towns two negro men gave us a cursing and called us "poor white trash" and pretended they were going to ride over the wagon. I couldn't blame the boys much. We surely did look pretty tough. But mother couldn't stand it. She got the old musket out of the back end of the wagon and loaded it up. She put in a hand full of powder, put a wad of paper in on it and beat it down with the ramrod, then put in sixteen buckshot and a little paper on that. While she was getting the box of caps the colored boys had business up the lane. I tell you mother was one of the pluckiest little rebels you ever saw.

Lee surrendered in 1865, but it was many years later when Mother Robinson surrendered. I think she could see blue-coats and muskets in her dreams, until the year Bros. H. C. Morrison and Joe McClurkan held the Waco Holiness Camp Meeting, when mother got so happy in the experience of full salvation that she lost her little black bonnet, her handbag and her prejudice, and hasn't seen the Mason and Dixon line since.

CHAPTER III.

We reached the mountains of Tennessee just before Christmas in 1869 and settled in a little cove or valley between two great mountains. Here we made headquarters until 1876. The mountain life is a very peculiar one. A fellow has to live there to understand the situation. Thirty odd years ago the mountains surely were a rough place. We had almost as great a war in 1872 and 1873 as we did in 1862 and 1863, when Uncle Sam was setting the negroes free. In '72 and '73 he was collecting the revenue on whisky and brandy. You see, we mountaineers made corn whisky for 25 cents per gallon and apple brandy for 50 cents per gallon, and of course when Uncle Sam came in and put a revenue on corn whisky of 50 cents and apple brandy of 75 cents per gallon, when we were only getting 25 cents for whisky and 50 cents for brandy, he met a hostile people. There was war as soon as the first officer arrived. Those mountaineers clubbed together, and got in their old log houses with their muskets and citizens' rifles. If you don't think they killed men by the hundreds, you ask Uncle Sam. Within five miles of our house there were ten stills

27

running day and night the year round, and of course the country was flooded with whisky. The whisky peddlers called at our door every day, and with their ox cart loaded with whisky sold it out for country produce—chickens, eggs, corn, potatoes, or anything the people raised. We bought and used it like milk and thought it was the remedy for every disease known to the human family. A man couldn't be born, married or die without it, and every boy in the country was drunk two or three times a week, and we thought nothing of it. From the time little boys were ten years old they were getting drunk.

Churches or schools were almost a thing unknown at that time. Civilization had not then reached the mountains. Railroads, steam engines, buggies or carriages, and houses of lumber were things unknown in my boyhood days. Our houses were made of logs and the cracks between were daubed with mud. Our chimneys were made of sticks and mud. The floors were made of puncheons, or dirt, without a window in the house. The roofing was of oak boards, three or four feet long, split out by hand. Our hauling was done on sleds and ox carts. Our breadstuff was made at the little water mill down the creek, where we boys used to go and stay almost all day waiting for our turn, as it would take from two to three hours to grind one sack of corn. We boys would spend the time in fishing, playing marbles or talking with the old men.

Our clothing was homemade. Mother spun and wove our clothes and made every garment we wore, by hand. I was a grown man when I first saw a sewing machine. Mother wove jeans every fall to make our winter clothing, and cotton checks and cottonades every spring for shirts and pants. When we had shoes mother knit our socks, but we were not troubled with shoes often. I had only worn out about one pair when I was big enough to go to see the girls, and the girls in the mountains of Tennessee were as bad off as we boys. They did not have their little feet all cramped up with shoe leather, so we just sparked barefooted and had no idea we needed shoes to spark in. We were all on the same platform, and such a thing as going to church or Sunday school never entered our heads.

I was a man with beard on my face the first Sunday school I ever saw. There were but few people that could read or write among the poorer people, and morality was at a very low ebb. The most of the young women were raising families "without the incumbrance of a husband." It was a very common thing when a neighbor called for him to ask if "you had heard that John and Sal had 'took up' together." This was their style of matrimony. Without the expense

of a license or a preacher they just "took up together."
"John and Sal" might be a boy and girl, or perhaps
the father and mother in different families that lived
in the neighborhood, and they seemed to be about as
well respected as anybody else. I have been in homes
where the mother had eleven or twelve children, their
oldest daughter three children, the second daughter
two, the third one child, and the whole family would
live in from one to two little rooms, made of logs with
dirt floor and from one to two old bedsteads, without
a cooking stove. One or two chairs and an old bench
constituted the furniture, but any number of neighbors
were pressed to spend the night and often accepted the
proffered hospitality. Some one will say, "Where on
earth did that crowd sleep?" Well, now, reader, that
is a secret that belongs to us mountain folks. But if
you will promise never to tell anybody I will make it
so plain to you that you can never forget it.

Now, did you ever throw down four or five old
sheep skins and an old quilt or two and just see how
many children you could put down on them? "Well,"
you say, "but what did they do for pillows?" Well,
now, friend, if you go to wanting pillows you had better stay out of the mountains of Tennessee.

There was but little money in circulation at that
time. In fact, we did not need much money—there

was little to buy in the country. The men tanned their leather and made their own shoes at home, the women made the clothing, and the people raised everything they ate. We raised corn and wheat, potatoes, cabbage, fruit and berries in great quantities. Our hogs got fat every fall on the acorns and chestnuts in the mountains, and our 'possums got fat on the persimmons. We generally lived on 'possum most of the fall season. The young man that couldn't twist a 'possum out of a hollow log and dress him nice was no catch at all with the mountain girls, and the boy who had a good 'possum dog was considered first choice. I want the reader to remember now and forever hereafter that in my day on the old Cumberland mountains there was nothing in this world equal to 'possum and sweet potatoes. You see, we had great big fireplaces six or seven feet long, and we would roll on a great back log two feet through, put on a big forestick and then pile on a big lot of little wood and just build up a log heap. We then dressed the old 'possum nice, put him into an old-fashioned oven, put the fire all around him and bring in a peck of yellow yam potatoes, put them in the fire and cover them up with hot ashes. We children would sit up, tell riddles and play blindfold until the old 'possum would get done.

Now, reader, just think of our satisfaction as mother

takes the lid off the oven and we smell the 'possum and see him brown and juicy in the big old oven, and mother takes him out on the big dish and we proceed to take out the potatoes. Of course, supper is now ready, and all hands go to work. We don't stop to ask a blessing. We had given thanks when we had caught the 'possum.

Supper being over, such a thing as family prayer never being heard of in our country, we had nothing to do but to go to bed. We were not troubled with getting clean sheets and pillow slips. We just bring a sheep skin out of the corner and spread it out before the fire and lie down, and in a few minutes we are in the land of delight, and dreaming some of the finest things that ever passed through the mind of a mountain boy.

About this time in my life an impression was made on my mind I never forgot. I went to spend the night with a little boy who had a religious home. I had never been in a religious home. This was a good man and his home was a religious one, and they had plenty to eat, nice white linen tablecloth on the table and plenty of dishes. He asked a blessing at the table and he helped the plates of his wife and children; he helped me. I had never seen anything of that kind before. After supper we played blindfold and popped corn, roasted potatoes and ate apples and had a fine time until bedtime. The father then told the children it was time for bed and then he told them all to sit down quietly, and he took down an old book from the shelf and he talked out of it a long time. I did not know what he was at, as I had never seen family worship in my life. All got down on their knees and I knelt with them. The father talked just like he loved everybody and I knew that he was talking to the Lord, and after he had talked to Him a while about his wife and all of his children he began to talk to Him about me. I was so glad I was there, and that he was talking to the Lord about me and many things I never will forget. He asked the Lord to help me and to take care of me and to put his arms around me and make me a blessing to my home and to the world.

It touched my little heart. I said right then that when I got to be a man I was going to have me a nice home, a wife and children, and I would be kind to my wife and children, ask a blessing at the table, read the Bible and pray and let my children eat apples, play, and have a nice time in my home.

Well, I thank God I have lived to see that desire that sprung up in my heart fulfilled. While I am writing, two of the sweetest babies on earth are playing around me and pulling at my coat skirts and saying,

"Papa, come and swing me," and their mamma looks on and smiles.

Now, it seemed so sad to me to go from this home of kindness and family prayers, back to our old log cabin and hear nothing but cursing and quarreling, but such was my fate. That was in 1872. In that year my father died, leaving mother in the mountains with ten children, but few friends and no money. Bless her old soul, I don't see how she lived and kept the children alive. But I remember now, she would spin all day and then weave until midnight.

My father had been in the whisky business, he had squandered his fortune, wrecked his life and mother's heart was broken and we were started in the wrong direction. Of course, there is nothing worse than a home wrecked by whisky. The man loses all his friends and his wife and children are without friends and without money and without education or without anything that would commend them to the world only their need. I have had many people make fun of me for the way I was brought up. They never did tell me how to find Jesus, nor how to get shoes when I was barefooted. So life was a drudge and a burden from the first of my recollections. By the time I was 12 years old my whole family had gone into the lowest life in the world. My oldest brothers were getting

drunk every week and my two sisters were in bad company two or three nights in the week.

Our old cabin was full of drunken boys three or four
nights in each week. The young men that came to see
my sisters would come so drunk they could not get off
their horses, and we would have to help them off when
they came and help them on when they left. Whisky
was as common as water, and we didn't know any better than to get drunk at everything we did. I was
the only one of the family of eight that would never
drink. My home was a hell on earth. We cursed and
swore and fought, and our home was one of the saddest
places in the world. God somehow kept me from doing many things I saw others do. Father and brothers
were drunk much of the time. When a young couple
was married, whisky was used. It was used for the
different purposes of life. Father died a pauper, of
course, and the neighbors had to bury him. If he was
saved, it was during the last hour he lived in the
world. Nothing on earth is worse than the life of a
whisky-cursed man. Hell is but little worse. So at
the age of sixty he had squandered his fortune, and
had wrecked his life. At one time he was in the height
of prosperity and paid the highest taxes of any man in
the community. He was an educated man, but the
brainy man will go down as quick as the ignorant man.

Sin will wreck any man on the face of the earth. Our home was without religious training; such a thing as going to church and school was unheard of.

Now, reader, you have a faint picture of the mountain life and it is not overdrawn, for our house was looked upon as one of the nicest places in the community, and we struggled on in that way until the fall of '76, when my mother sold out what little she had there and moved to Texas. We settled in Dallas county, near Lancaster, rented a farm and made a crop on the halves, the man furnishing teams, feed and farming implements. We made a fine crop, but we did not know how to sell cotton and get the money, for none of us boys could read or write, and didn't know how to transact business. The man took advantage of our ignorance and swindled us out of almost everything we made that year.

We boys then began to scatter out and leave home. I hired out that winter to a man and worked for him three years—until the summer of 1880, when God converted me.

CHAPTER IV.

I was converted on the 11th of August, 1880, Wednesday, about 11 o'clock at night. That was the grandest time in all my life. It is as bright and clear in my mind today as if it had been but a few hours ago.

A Methodist preacher had come through the country and arranged to hold a camp meeting about twelve miles from where we lived. My mother arranged to go and planned for me to go with her.

Well, Glory to God for being brought in touch with the Almighty. A man never forgets the first time he met the Lord, and He lifts His blessed face on him full of tenderness and compassion. It makes an impression on him that will last throughout an endless eternity, and he feels his sins rolling away and rivers of salvation running down out of the clouds through his soul. The change is so wonderful—brought from the bottom to the top in the twinkling of an eye. In a single moment he is changed from a pauper to the son of God. I will never forget that night. I went there without a friend, but mother. I was a walking tramp, but went back an heir to God—a joint heir

38

with Jesus Christ and my name written in Heaven.

How wonderfully God surprises people sometimes. I did not go to that meeting to get religion. Mother urged me two or three days to get me off and I only went there to have fun and a good time, but I just walked right into salvation. Well, praise the Lord forever! It was God's way to reach me. Mother didn't know I had cards or an old pistol, but the Lord did.

I walked about the camp ground two or three days trying to get a number of boys to play cards with me. But it seemed to me everybody was talking about religion. This was my first trip to a Methodist camp meeting. It was the old Bluff Spring camp ground on the line between Dallas and Ellis counties. I had been there a day or two when the Christians were all sent back into the congregation to pray with some one, and an old lady that looked to be nearly a hundred years old came to the back bench and found me. She knelt down before me and placed her hands on my knees. She asked God to stop me and not let me walk right into an awful hell. She seemed to tell the Lord all about me. I feel sure some one had told her. I at first wanted to run, then I felt like getting mad, and so I got into an awful fix. I stayed through the prayer and by that time God had hold of me.

That night they put up a little dried-up looking

preacher with a short coat on to preach, and I thought the whole thing would be a failure. But he hadn't preached twenty minutes until he had knocked every prop from under me, and I found my infidelity floating away. The man I worked with for three years was a Universalist, and he had filled my head with universalism and infidelity, but when that old preacher held up Jesus Christ as the friend of lost sinners and the Saviour of the world I forgot everything but my awful condition. I sat there and wept while he preached. At the opening I had taken a seat on the back bench by a little red-headed girl that was a great dancer, and thought I would have a nice night of it, but in a few minutes I was under such awful conviction I forgot to spark the girl. When the altar call was made a great many went. I sort of held back, but pretty soon an old preacher came down the aisle and asked me if there was a young man back there who wanted to meet him in heaven? If so, to come and give him his hand. I thought if I was ever going to do anything religious now was my time. I got up and started to give him my hand. By the time I got to the preacher I was weeping aloud, and the sins of my whole life were standing up before me.

I had a pistol and a pack of cards in my pocket. I had on a pair of old, greasy overalls, my old blue hick-

BUD, THE TEXAS COWBOY.

ory shirt was torn at the elbows and the buttons were all off in front. As I went by the old man caught my hand and shook it. Every step down the aisle I felt like I was walking right into an awful hell. The old pistol in my pocket felt as big as a mule and the pack of cards felt as heavy as a bale of cotton. I met the devil in the aisle and he tried to keep me from going to the altar. He told me that people would make fun of my greasy breeches, and my dirty shirt. I right then lost confidence in the devil. He had put the old dirty clothes on me, and as I had started to get new ones the devil tried to keep me from going. Then the devil came up and said, "Everybody will know that you have got a deck of cards and a pistol." The old rascal! I had got them both from him, and now when I wanted to get something better he made fun of me. When I reached the altar it was full. I never heard such weeping and praying before in all my life. Somebody said: "Fix this young man a seat; he is deeply struck." I didn't need a seat—I only needed room to fall. I fell on my face, stretched in the altar. The good people gathered around me. It seemed to me fifty people were praying for me. You could have heard them a half mile away. I felt like I was right over hell on a broken rail and would be dead and in hell in another minute. I was praying at the top of my voice for God to keep me out of hell.

As I was lying there in the straw my whole life of sin came up before me. The lies that I had told seemed to have stingers in them like bald-headed hornets, and they were stinging a guilty conscience. If you have never been a barefooted boy in the mountains of Tennessee and thrown a rock into a bald-headed hornets' nest and have them run you a hundred yards and sting you right in the back as you got in under a brush pile, my friend, you don't know what bald-headed hornets are. The oaths that I had uttered seemed to have teeth in them and were biting pieces out of my guilty conscience. All the watermelons I had stolen seemed to be piled up around me and their striped backs were grinning in my face and they said, "You got me," and I said, "Yes, but I am done." And every grass-sack of peaches I had stolen, seemed to be lying right across my stomach and holding me down to the earth. Just then it seemed that a landslide from the New Jerusalem struck me in the soul and I have never seen the watermelons, lies or oaths or those old sacks of peaches from that day to this. The Lord has supplied me with watermelons and peaches, Bless His dear name.

It seemed to me that all that Heaven is or all that Heaven means broke in on my soul, and I was flooded with light and glory and was in a new world. The sinner and the Christian live in countries millions of miles apart.

The people looked like angels. I never saw such a change in people before or since. Just before midnight I came to myself, and I was walking the backs of the benches shouting and praising God, and the Lord only knows what I didn't do. Well, Glory to God forever. It never grows old, and is always fresh and juicy.

What a step I took that night! I stepped from nothing to everything. I went out and unloaded. Nobody had told me to unload, but somehow when a fellow gets religion he naturally unloads. I threw my old pistol into the thicket and burned my cards in an old camp fire and lay down under a wagon and put my old hat on a mesquite stump for a pillow, but sleep, oh my! I never thought of going to sleep. The Lord marched out all the stars of heaven on a dress parade for my special benefit, and the stars leaped, and hopped and skipped and jumped and turned somersaults and clapped their hands and laughed all night. The Lord showed me that it was all at His expense and did not cost me one nickel. I just lay there and laughed and just watched the stars as they were playing up and down the milky way. The Lord met me that night under the old wagon and told me He wanted me to preach, and I told Him I would do anything He wanted done; but, oh my! I did not know what I was going to get into.

The next morning I went up to what they call a testimony meeting. I had never seen or been in one before. One man got up and told what God had done for him and how He had saved him. While he was telling it I was so happy I had to hold to the bench to keep down. I waited for two or three to talk. Pretty soon I got up to tell my experience. I was so full I felt like I could ride off on the clouds. I was so happy I did not know anything in the world, and I just threw my arms around a great big post and pretty soon I began to climb to the top of the post, and the people in the audience were not behaving any better than I was. Everybody got to shouting. Heaven came down on earth and the rejoicing lasted for hours.

The minister then opened the doors of the church and the people marched up to join. I had never seen anybody join a church and did not know what they had to do, but I fell in line and marched up with the crowd and the preacher took me by the hand and said: "What church do you want to join?" And I said, "How many have you got?" And he said, "Well, we have the Methodist, Baptist and Presbyterian." (It was a union meeting.) I said, "Which one are you in?" He said, "I am a Methodist preacher and on this work." I said, "I want you to put me in the same one that you are in," and he said, "All right."

Then he said, "How do you want to be baptized?" I said, "How do you fix a fellow when he is baptized?" He said, "Some want to be immersed; we just take a fellow down to the creek and put him under the water; some want the water sprinkled on them; others want the preacher to take a pitcher and glass and pour clean water in it and pour it on his head. I told him I wanted to be fixed in that way. Of course, I was fixed that way. So while he was pouring clean water on me, I was shouting as loud as I could and I have not stopped yet.

Well, glory to God, friends! Getting religion is one of the finest things in the world. The man who gets it is surely ahead. I would rather see people get religion than anything I ever saw or heard of in all this old world.

I could not read or write at that time, although twenty years old. I soon went to my first Sunday school in my life. A young lady gave me a little Testament and I commenced to spell in the first chapter of Matthew's Gospel. I found it awful hard spelling; it looked to me like I never would learn to read in the world, but the Lord helped me and by the time I had spelled over to the Sermon on the Mount, I found that I could read the easiest words. I did not know it was the Sermon on the Mount.

I went to work then at 50 cents a day, grubbing mesquite stumps and eating corn bread and sorghum molasses and drinking tank water. When I had eaten my breakfast, I would feel as if I would never want any more bread and molasses, but by noon I would find I was hungry again. Many times I have sat down and would put my feet into the hole where I dug out the stumps and lean back against the stump and eat my bread and molasses and take out my Testament and read two or three chapters and then pray and the Lord would bless me wonderfully there. There is nothing finer than bread and molasses when Jesus is with you, blessing your soul. Well, Glory to God for a salvation that will reach you when everything else fails.

After I was saved it was not long until the Lord put it into my heart to rescue and save my brothers. They were all very wicked and drank and used tobacco and were profane swearers and seemed to take no interest in their own salvation. I prayed for them for several years before they seemed to yield and come to the Lord. I have gone to town and would haul them home in a two-horse wagon so drunk that they could not get up. I would unload them and sit up with them during the night and pray with them and keep them from fighting with each other. After many years' struggling and praying, the Lord saved my two youngest brothers, and in a short time after they were saved, He called them to preach. They worked for the Lord a few years and were very faithful and true and were filled with the Holy Ghost. Right in the bloom of youth they both died and both went to Heaven, praising God. My two oldest brothers ran on for several years. The oldest was the worst drunkard and opium eater I ever saw. The Lord has saved him and cleaned him up and he is now preaching the Gospel. My second oldest brother was a great sinner, but he did not use tobacco or opium, and he has been wonderfully saved, and he is now one of the finest Christian workers I ever saw. He preaches in the mills and shops, up and down the country. When he goes to town, or to the mill, or to the cotton gin, while he is waiting for his cotton to be ginned, he will preach to the men in the gin yard. When he goes to the mill, while his corn is being ground he prays with the miller, and tells the mill hands his experience, and what a great sinner he has been and how God has wonderfully saved him and gloriously sanctified him and filled him with the Holy Ghost. He is uneducated;

he cannot write, but he can read in the New Testament and he can shout and exhort and bring many people to Christ. He is a useful man in his country and a blessing to the whole community where he lives.

Bud and His Pony

CHAPTER V.

CALLED TO PREACH.

Soon after my conversion the Lord told me that it was time to go to preaching. The Lord met with me and told me that I had agreed under the wagon that I would preach; now he said you must go at it. I had no books but my little Testament and a young man had given me a Prayer and Praise song book—that was my whole library. My clothes were the very cheapest that could be bought. I bought cheap cotton cloth and mother made me some pants and a coat and bought speckled calico at a nickel a yard and made me a Sunday shirt. I had cheap plow shoes and a two-bit straw hat; that made up my wardrobe. My old pony was not worth $10, and people would tell me that it would not bring $5.00 on the market, but I would stutter and try to tell them that it was not for sale, I had to ride it to go preaching. My rope-rein bridle and old saddle were not worth over $2.00. The first year I preached the Lord gave me about 300 conversions.

When I felt that I must preach I first spoke to one of the stewards of the church, and he told me that I stuttered so bad and had so little sense, I would bring reproach on the church and do more harm than good.

I cried about it and thought I had better not try it, but the Lord met me and told me that I had promised Him to preach when I was under the wagon, now I had to go at it. I went to see another man, that was, I thought, a good friend, and told him of my awful struggles in my heart, but he said: "You will have to teach in Sunday school and lead prayer meetings. For the Lord's sake, don't you ever try to preach." I never will forget this man. My poor heart was struggling and the Lord said you must preach and the men said you can't and you must not try it, and I did not know what to do. I then went to see an old local preacher. After we had eaten dinner we walked together down below his little barn, and I told him that I had something in my heart that I wanted to tell him. I had made up my mind that if he advised me as the other men did that I never would try to preach in the world. But he took me by the hand and said, "Brother, I know the struggles of your heart, the Lord has called you to preach and you are trying to get out of it, because some of the brethren think that you can't do it." He said, "the first time I ever saw you and heard you pray I knew that God had called you to preach." He helped me out of my difficulty. He said, "The Quarterly Conference meets in two weeks and I will put your case before the church this afternoon and get

Bud, the Texas Preacher

a recommendation to the Quarterly Conference."
That afternoon he put my case before the house and
had me to go out. He told me that all the religious
people and all the sinners voted for me to get license
to exhort, and when he told me about it I could not
keep from shouting and praising God. In about two
weeks the Presiding Elder came around and I went
before the Conference to be examined. I answered
nary a question he asked me. He asked me about my
schooling and my grammar, and I had never studied
it at all. He asked me about the laws of the Church
and the rules of discipline and I had never seen a
discipline or studied one in my life, did not know
what they were for. I stuttered so bad I could not
tell him my name or what I wanted to do, and he
looked at me and twisted his mustache and run his
hands through his hair, and said, "Well, you must step
aside a little while." After I was called in
the Presiding Elder told me that when I was out
they had acted on my case, and had decided to give
me license to exhort. One of my friends told me
privately that they said that I could not preach, and
would never try it, but I was little, and ignorant, and
afflicted, and it would dishearten me if they did not
give me license, and I would do no harm if I did have

it, and for my sake they would give them to me to satisfy me.

I got my license and started out at once preaching the gospel. From the time I was converted I went to work for the Lord, praying, preaching and exhorting up and down the settlement, and holding meetings at night and seemed to preach as well before I got the license as I did afterwards, and apparently done as much good.

Sometimes when I started out to preach I would go twelve or fifteen miles to a school house. I stuttered so bad I could not ask the way to a place. I once rode up to a man's fence and called out, hello. When the man came out I tried to ask him how to get to a school house, but as I couldn't tell him who I was, nor the name of the place I wanted to go to, I would open my mouth and stutter, and nod my head and point in the direction I wanted to go, and he would begin to ask me if it was this place or that, and finally he would call the name of the place and I could nod my head and tell him yes, that was the place I was trying to go to.

When I undertook to explain anything, I could not say anything but when I got up and forgot everything, my mouth would open and God would fill it and I would begin to exhort.

The first four years that I preached the people gave me $16.00, which would make $4.00 a year. I remember once going about 20 miles from home to preach and nobody asked me home with them all night, and I staked out my pony that night on the ground and slept on a bench, and the next morning when people came in to preaching one man said to me, "Brother Bud you got here early this morning," and I said, "Yes, I got here yesterday." He said, "Well where did you stay last night?" I said, "Right here on this bench." He seemed to be surprised that nobody had asked me home with them, and after I had preached that morning he kneeled at the altar, and the Lord blessed his soul, and I had a place to go after that.

When I was first licensed to exhort, the Presiding Elder told me when he gave me the license, that I should keep a record of every sermon that I preached, and every prayer meeting that I held, and every house I prayed in and the number of people that God saved under my preaching and come to the next Quarterly Conference and read my report. When I went up to the next Quarterly Conference I had held twenty-seven prayer meetings, I had tried to preach fifty times, I had prayed in ninety-five homes and had about sixty people converted. When I got to the Quar-

terly Conference and was called on for my report I
got up and tried to read it and couldn't—I broke down
and commenced to cry and I got to shouting and the
Presiding Elder came and got the report and read
it to the Quarterly Conference. He told me that it
was an unusually good report, that the Lord was with
me, and that I should keep on. That was my first
report to a Quarterly Conference.

When I had preached two years as a licensed ex-
horter, I went to my first District Conference. We
had a great time. The brethren put me up to preach
and I cried and exhorted and shouted for over an
hour, and called mourners to the altar. It was filled
and there were more than twenty people converted.
After that the preachers commenced to send for me to
come and hold meetings for them.

For a number of years I preached on Sunday and
then would hold revivals during the summer when our
crops were laid by. I would generally put in about
three months in holding protracted meetings. The
rest of the time I worked on a farm, and bought a
farm of my own and had it nearly paid for when I
was sanctified.

CHAPTER VI.

BUD AND THE OLD MAN.

I had ten years of struggle with the old man—or what is called the "ups and downs" of a Christian life without the fullness of Christ.

I was converted in August, 1880. I received the blessing of a clean heart in 1890.

Getting wholly sanctified does not mean getting religion over again, or reclamation from a state of backsliding. A regenerated man is a Christian, and a Christian is a child of God, but with all that, there is something in the heart of an unsanctified man that causes him a world of trouble. It would be for our good and for God's glory for us to confess up and go down before God and get the old man crucified.

I meet with thousands of people who claim that they don't need anything after conversion. I am sure I did, and if you love me like you will have to love me to get to heaven, you ought to be willing for me to get it as soon as possible after I find out there is a something in my heart that conversion did not cure— pride, selfishness, jealousy, fretfulness, peevishness, self-will, ambition, anger, wrath, malice—these are some of the enemies that are not killed in conversion, and I struggled with this something for ten years.

Now, my friend, if you have never been troubled with any of these things since you were converted, I say, amen, to it; you have been more fortunate than I.

When we used to meet at the little church or school house to have our weekly prayer meetings we would open up by singing,

"Prone to wander, Lord, I feel it,
Prone to leave the God I love."

Then some brother would be called on to lead the meeting. He would throw his tobacco out of his mouth and say, "Let us pray;" then he would get down on his knees and say, "Oh, Lord, I am a sinner in Thy sight and am not worthy to take Thy Holy name between my sin-polluted lips. I do many things I ought not to do and leave undone many things I ought to do, and am a poor weak worm of the dust." As he would say, "Amen!" we would sing:

"Show pity, Lord; oh Lord, forgive,"
"Let a repenting rebel live,"

have another prayer and sing:

"I saw a way-worn traveler
    In tattered garments clad,
And struggling up the mountain
    It seemed that he was sad."

Then the leader would say: "Who will be first to take up his cross and tell how he is getting along?" Some old brother would get up and throw a big chew of tobacco over into the corner and say: "Well, brethren, I am like everybody else; I am having my ups and downs in life; when I would do good, evil is present with me, and I find Jordan is a hard road to travel. I have had more ups and downs this week than I ever had in my life. I have been mad enough to die all week, and I want all to pray for me that I may hold out to the end." Then we would sing, "Climbing up Zion's hill." And the leader would say: "Now come along with your testimonies, take up your cross; who will be the next?" and some old sister would get up with her mouth full of snuff and tell of her trials, temptations and hardships, and not one in the crowd would praise God for a thing in the world. We only went there, it seemed, to be together, chew tobacco, dip snuff and tell of our defeats. Not one would tell of a single victory he had had.

The reader must remember that the conditions and surroundings were very different then to what they are now up and down the country. It was a common thing for all the men to chew tobacco and the women to dip snuff, and their piety as true Christians was not questioned at all. It was just as common to see this thing as to breathe. We had no idea that it was wrong. Horse racing was practiced all over the settlement and no one thought that it was a great sin to attend horse races, as people went whether they gambled or not, and we thus paid little attention to such things.

After my conversion I ran on three months without a break in my religious experience, and the same grace that flowed through my heart that night under the old wagon, seemed to flow up and down through my soul, but one night I went to sleep, praying, and slept off my religion. When I woke up the next morning it was gone, and I did not know what to do about it. When I woke up I had the blues, I tried to pray and the skies over my head were brass, and the Lord wouldn't listen to me. I got on my old pony and rode across the country four or five miles, and told one of the stewards of the church that I was ruined, that I had lost my religion. He said, "Well, how in the world did you lose it?" I said, "I slept it off last night." He said, "When did you have it last?" I told him I had it when I went to sleep last night. He said, "How in the world did you get rid of it?" I told him it was gone when I woke up this morning. He said, "Have you been praying?" I said, "Yes, and the Lord has been a hearing me when

I talked, but he quit to-day, and I don't know what to do about it." "Well," he said, "Brother Bud you are having your doubts now." I said, "What on earth are they?" I didn't know a religious fellow had any-thing like them. He then said, "When you were con-verted you didn't get the Old Adam took out and he's in there, and will stay till you die, and you can't get him out, but if you live faithful till death the Lord will give you a crown of life." "Oh! if he would just have told me that I could have got the "old man" out. How much he would have saved me, but he didn't seem to know it himself, and he couldn't lead me where he hadn't been. I went back home a sad boy. That night I could not sleep; the next morning I got up and went to the lot to feed the mules, and I got down behind a hay stack to pray and rolled around there for half an hour, and the Lord met me and seemed to give me back my religious joy again. I thought the thing was then settled forever; I didn't know I would ever have an-other religious spell, but to my surprise before I had run long one morning I wanted to do some work with one of my mules. I went and harnessed him up, and brought him out to the little yard fence, and tied him. I went into the house to do something and he broke the bridle and ran off across the pasture with the harness on. My hounds ran up and took after him, the other mule ran through the fence and broke the gate down, and the cow and calf got together. At last my temper commenced to pop out, and I stamped the ground, and pulled my hair, and wished for a cannon loaded with log chains to kill the mule and dogs with. After I had cooled off, up came the devil and said, "Well what did you do with your religion again?" and so there I was without any grace and the devil making fun of me. I did not know that there was anything in the world that would take out the thing that got up in my heart. I struggled on this way for several years. When I would make a break, then I would go to the Lord and weep over what I had done, and promise never to do it in the world again, and the Lord would forgive me and take me back.

Just before I was sanctified I was plowing in the field and plowed up till near noon. The mule wanted to go to dinner and I wanted to plow. He said he wouldn't plow any longer, and I said he would. I whipped him with the lines, and got where I could get him by the bridle bits and jerked him and then kicked him as long as I could raise my feet, and ran back and grabbed the plow handle and tried to make him go, but he wouldn't do it. I finally grabbed him by the bridle bits and twisted his nose with one hand, and reached up and got hold of his ear and pulled it down, and began to bite the end of his ear. He threw me to the ground and nearly knocked the breath out of me, and ran off with the plow and broke the handles off. I went up the hill pulling mule hairs out from between my teeth, and I said, "Well he didn't plow, but I got satisfaction out of him." That was on Saturday and I had to preach the next day, and as I walked up the hill the devil said, "What are you going to preach about tomorrow. What are you going to tell the Lord can do for a fellow?" I had to hunt a place to pray and promised the Lord if he would pardon again and restore to me the joys of salvation, and give me victory in my soul again I would never more grieve him. I would think I had the thing settled forever, but only to run a short time and meet with another defeat.

Just a week or two before I was sanctified I was going to preach one Sunday morning and studied my sermon as I was riding along. My pony stumbled and I grabbed the bridle reins and jerked it, and hit him over the head with my fist. By the time I had cooled off up came the devil and said, "Well, what subject are you going to preach on today?" I had to tie up my pony and hunt another place to pray, and get right with the Lord before I could go on to meet the crowd awaiting me at the school house.

One trouble I had in my justified life was with jealousy. I sent for a young man to help me hold a meeting at one of my preaching places where I had built up a nice little church. He was a fine young man, and a good friend of mine, and I loved him tenderly and we were like brothers. While we were holding the meetings, because he could preach better than I could, the devil came up and said, "If you let this man preach a better sermon than you can preach, the people will want him to preach here instead of you," and I became so jealous of him that before the meeting was over, I nearly hated him in my heart. The devil told me that if I didn't preach as good a sermon as this young man that I would lose my place there. I went home and wrote out a sermon and memorized it, and went back to my next monthly appointment to preach a sermon as well as my friend, and to show the people that I could sermonize too. When I went back to preach my sermon I got up and gave out my hymn; I then stepped up from behind a little table that was in the middle of the room in the old school house and undertook to say my speech, and by the time I had talked five minutes I had forgotten the whole thing and could not remember any of it at all. And then I thought I would preach a sermon like I had been preaching and I couldn't think of anything to say, and I saw that I had lost the whole thing and the only thing was to dismiss the congregation. As I had forgotten the benediction, I finally had to tell them just to go home. Everybody looked at me very strangely and nobody asked me home with them but one old man, a hard-shelled Baptist, but I told him I couldn't stay, I had to go home; but I had gone down there to stay two days and nights with them, but when I failed on my sermon, I had to leave the settlement. I rode out a mile or two from the school house, and rode off into a thicket and tied my pony and got down in a brush thicket, and asked God to forgive me for being the biggest fool on earth and that if he would forgive me I never would do that way any more.

I prayed there for at least two hours and I had a fearful struggle with the "old man."

CHAPTER VII.

Six years after my conversion, Brother W. B. Godbey came to our home town, Alvarado, Texas, to hold a meeting. The word went out over the country that he was a sanctified man. We had no idea what a sanctified man looked like and, of course, everybody in the country went to hear him. He preached on hell, and said that all sinning religion would land the people right into an awful hell, and of course war broke out in the community, and you never heard such tales on earth as were told on that old man.

But he never stopped or let up. He preached on hell until the people screamed and held to their benches. He ran the meeting a month, and over two hundred and fifty were converted and sanctified. I went to hear him and thought I understood the whole matter. I thought he was crazy and would be in the asylum before the meeting closed. He said we would have to give up tobacco or stay out of Heaven; that we could not go into Heaven with a chew of "Star Navy" in our mouths. Circus and theater-goers and horse-racers were not on the road to Heaven at all. This to us was a new doctrine—the idea of a man having to give up tobacco and horse racing to get to Heaven! To my amazement I commenced to feel like it was so, and to my surprise I found myself under conviction for a clean heart, but by this time the meeting had closed and I had to struggle on for four years longer.

The next year after Brother Godbey's meeting Brother Ben Gassaway was our pastor. The life he lived and the sermons he preached sealed Brother Godbey's doctrine. The seed that were sown in my heart that year kept perfectly sound for four years. The devil covered the seed up with the clods of unbelief and told me every seed had rotted.

But Bless the Lord! On the 7th of June, 1890, a tree of perfect love sprang up from the bottom of my soul with sanctification written all over it, grapes and pomegranates on every limb and honey dripping from the leaves. Glory to God, Holiness seed never rots! It will keep for many years in any climate on earth and grow, as well in poor climate as rich. That is one of the peculiarities of Holiness seed. It will produce an abundant harvest in the poorest soil on earth. If the drought ruins the corn and the boll worm destroys the cotton, it doesn't affect the crop of Holiness at all. It grows and flourishes and yields a greater crop than under any other circumstances. I have seen Holiness seed in the mud just as sound as a dollar and I have seen it in the dust growing and looking as fresh and beautiful as if it had been planted on the banks of a running stream. When the seed gets planted once in a community there is no way on earth to stop it. It is like Johnson grass—it just simply takes the country. This is one of the reasons the enemies of Holiness hate it so bad. There is no chance to kill it out. If they pull up one, a dozen will come up in its place. You see the thing that makes some people awfully mad, makes others shout. The idea of not being able to kill it out nearly tickles me to death.

Well, Glory!

There is something about getting sanctified a fellow never forgets. I remember now the morning I went down into my field to thin corn—it was on Monday morning. I had preached twice on Sunday and told the people I was not sanctified, but wanted to be, worse than anything on earth. At night I called mourners for the blessing of sanctification and an old Presbyterian Elder met me at the altar, and I prayed for him and he prayed for me, but neither of us got victory that night. After preaching was over, I went home with him and stayed with him all night. We talked of the experience of sanctification until midnight. He said his church called it, "Rest of

Faith", but it was the same thing that I had preached about and that he wanted it.

On Monday morning I rode over home real early, turned my pony out in the pasture, put on my working clothes; by that time mother had breakfast ready. I ate my breakfast, got my hoe and went to work. I had a few hills of corn that needed thinning and the big weeds to be burned up, and I wanted to go down there and talk with the Lord. I had not thinned corn long until I commenced to preach to myself from the text, "Follow peace with all men, and Holiness without which no man shall see the Lord." I felt as if I could not live any longer in the condition I was in, and preach the Gospel. I told the Lord I must have help. I would thin corn a while and then get down and pray a while, and then get up and preach to myself again. I didn't get much corn thinned, and while I prayed I could hear my brothers driving their teams, and their cultivators rattling as they plowed cotton, but finally I got to a place where I did not hear anything that was going on around me, only the devil telling me I never would get the blessing. At last I got up and stood with my hoe in my hand. My hoe was the last thing I turned loose. As a result, I have never been troubled with a hoe from that day to this. About the time I turned my hoe loose the Lord came very near to me, and it seemed I could hardly stand on the earth, and the Lord was drawing so near me I could feel His presence. He just emptied me of everything, and as burning power went through me and swept out everything. I could see salvation rolling over the cornfield; it seemed to me I could see God's face shining on the corn blades—the corn was up in swab tassel, and all over the corn seemed to be rivers of grace. As the Lord went through me and took things out of my heart I did not know were in it, I felt that there was nothing left of me, and a peace that passes understanding flowed into my heart—the deepest, sweetest peace I had ever known. It just satisfied every craving of the mind and every longing of the soul; the waves became so great that I fell down and lay stretched out on the ground, while tidal waves of grace and billows of glory flowed through my whole being. Indeed it is the fulness of joy—the soul rest—the full assurance—perfect love—the baptism with the Holy Ghost—the destruction of the old man—or, the Second Blessing.

Well, Amen!

CHAPTER VIII.

THE HOLINESS WAR.

After the Lord sanctified me I supposed that everybody in the world would want the blessing. The first man I talked to about it was one of our stewards, and he said, "Brother Bud, you had better go mighty slow about this thing." I bless the Lord that he did not slow me up, but I didn't know then that I was going to meet with opposition after I was sanctified. I would go to town and meet the preachers on the sidewalk and they would stand and talk as long as I would stay, but after God gave me The Blessing, I would meet the same men when I would go over to our little town, and they would pass me on the sidewalk and just give me the ends of about two fingers and say, "Well, hello, Bud, I'll see you a little later on," but, bless your soul, they haven't seen me yet. I did not know that it was the blessing of Sanctification that was really separating us one from the other. I supposed that every man in the world would want what I had, but I found out differently. I never had any trouble in the church before I was sanctified. The brethren all seemed to want me, and after I got the blessing they commenced to turn the cold shoulder to me. Not long after my Sanctification my preacher advised me to go to school to South Western University, Georgetown, Texas. I entered school in the fall of '91 in my thirty-first year. As soon as I entered school I went to work with the boys and tried to get those that were unsaved saved, and I got the young men that were studying for the ministry santified. In a short time three others with my wife organized a Holiness prayer meeting. The Lord commenced to bless our prayer meetings, and save sinners and sanctified believers. This meeting has now been running for twelve years. Through this meeting a Holiness band has been organized and a Holiness camp meeting association formed. Hundreds and hundreds of souls have been brought to Christ through the influences of that Holiness prayer meeting.

I had not been in school long before I commenced to preach four or five times each week, and soon I was preaching from twenty to twenty-five times a month, and some days would pray in thirty-five homes. By April I had to throw my books down. I went out under the trees in the west part of the town and started a meeting among the poor people and forbid any of the rich people to come. We did not have any benches to sit on, we had no pulpit, or stand, or table, or anything of the kind. I stood on the ground and preached to the people sitting under the trees on the ground. The rich people commenced to come out and drive up close in their carriages. I told them that if they did not get out of their carriages and sit down on the ground with the rest of us I would move my meetings over to the field and would not be bothered with them. They said that if I would let them come, they would sit on the ground, and the Lord gave me a great revival there. That finished up my school work. I got my diploma in eight months and haven't used it any since.

When I got through school I started with the Presiding Elder and preached with him three months on Georgetown district. He sent over to St. Louis and got a large tent and held meetings three months, until I broke down. My health failed and I had to go home. We had hundreds of people saved. We did not hold a meeting in which there were less than one hundred and fifty souls saved.

I went on a year or two longer very peaceably, without any trouble that amounted to anything, but finally the Holiness War was opened up throughout the Southern Methodist Church, and one of the Bishops came out through Texas and said it would take five years to kill out the Holiness move, and commenced to try the preachers and located them against their protest

and drove out many of their best men. My Presiding
Elder forbid me to go out of town to preach, and the
preacher in charge forbid me to preach in town. Not
many months before that the Presiding Elder came
to me one day and said: "Where will you be tonight
at 8 o'clock?" I said, "I will be over here at a certain
home holding a Holiness prayer meeting." He said,
"Will you go with me to see a sick man?" I said,
"Yes." At 8 o'clock he drove up and called for me.
I got into the buggy with him and we drove out about
two miles from town. On the way out I said: "Who
is the man?" And he said, "I am the fellow; I have
come to the place where I have got to get the blessing
of sanctification." We drove up to the North Gabriel,
about two miles, into a big cedar grove, set in the
cliffs of the rocks. There I prayed with him that
night until half after one. God brought him up to
the light. He said that he knew his duty, but that if
he gave himself wholly to God and got sanctified he
would lose his place in the Conference, and could not
educate his children. He held a very prominent posi-
tion in Conference. From that night he commenced
to go back on God. I prayed with him five and a half
hours. A few months later the same man, at a
quarterly Conference tried me for my experience of
Sanctification one night five and a half hours. I prayed

with him from eight until half after one the next morning—five and one-half hours. He tried me from eight until half after one, five and a half hours. Then he said I would have to give up my conscience on the subject of sanctification as a second work of grace, or I would have to give up the Methodist Episcopal Church South. I told him as I didn't have but one conscience, and as there were many churches, I would keep my conscience. Being greatly urged, I withdrew from the M. E. Church South and at once wrote to the Presiding Elder of the M. E. Church to know if he would accept a man who believed in sanctification as a second blessing and had the thing, and he said he would; and I joined the M. E. Church, in which I hold membership at the present time.

After I had organized the Holiness prayer meeting it was not long until Miss Sallie Harper was blessedly sanctified and afterwards became my wife. She was one of the leading workers during our Holiness War in the town in which we lived. While I was trying to keep loyal to the church and while the Presiding Elder would not let me preach out of town, and the preacher in charge, in town, I ran a dye shop and wood wagon to support my family.

MRS. BUD ROBINSON
SALLIE (seven years old)   RUBIE (four years old)

CHAPTER IX.

The next eleven years were long and weary and full of toil and pain and disappointment—at times without money and no bread in the house, and thinly clad, my body undergoing the most excruciating pain it is possible for a man to pass through and live. For sixteen years I had occasionally epileptic fits, and for fifteen years I had paralysis, and for ten years bleeding of the lungs, and my arms had been several hundred times pulled out of place and put back.

This statement may seem extravagant, but it is literally true. Through the spasms that I had, a keen pain would strike me in the arms and they would be pulled out of joint. After a few years they would not stay in place, and if I reached up a little too high my arm would slip out of place, or if I reached a little too far back, it would come out of place. Or if in sneezing I threw up my hands, either one of my arms would come out of joint. When at work in the field and often at night in my sleep I would turn and throw my arms out of joint. Whenever my arms came out of place, I would have to lie down on my back and my brother would put his heel under my arm and get me by the wrist and pull it back in place. My arms finally got so bad that I had to leave them out of place because it was such intense suffering to have them coming out of place and then to have them pulled back in their right place again.

God is witness for those eleven years I had never had one doubt about the goodness and mercy of God and His power to save, sanctify and keep.

I believe every word of the Bible is true, and that God loves me. Jesus died for me and the Blessed Holy Ghost abides with me, the angels are watching over me, and, glory to God, some sweet day I am going to meet Jesus in the clouds, and live with Him forever.

In 1896 I was wonderfully healed by the Lord. He don't heal everybody. He knows they wouldn't glorify him. God wonderfully healed me of all, and clarified my mind, and gave me His word in my mind. He has helped me to understand His Word, and memorize it. Brethren, look after the poor, struggling little boys. In labors with others, I've seen in the last twenty years some 20,000 souls converted and sanctified. In 1890 I traveled 17,000 miles and saw some 5,000 converted and sanctified.

I ran for five years without a break and almost without a pain, but in 1901 I gave out. The dear Lord warned me almost every day for six weeks that I was working too hard. I was impressed that I must stop and take a rest, but I did not heed His voice. I broke down and my old trouble returned. I had four attacks in fifteen months. I spent most of the summer of 1902 at home resting, praying and loving God and every human being on earth. I felt that there was room in my heart for every poor, struggling son of Adam in our land. I never before had more faith in God than I had then. I believed that I would soon be strong enough to go on with my work. I felt as if God would let me stay here and love people for many years to come. If He did not, I felt as if it would be fine to have the blessed privilege of moving to Heaven.

Just think of a man coming from poverty, ignorance, disgrace, pain, misery and woe—getting into the chariot and riding through the skies, and sitting down on the banks of the river of life. Now, I earnestly ask every saint of God that reads this book to talk to the Lord about my health. I believe if I live a few years longer, I can love God and the people better and can be a greater blessing to the world than I have ever been.

I only want my health for God's glory—if it is not for my good and His glory I don't want to have it. I don't mind the suffering in the least; there is some-

thing about a pain in the head or back that makes a fellow feel that he is a dependent being upon an independent God. Without pain we would not know how frail the human family was nor how great God is. You sometimes see a strong, well man walking down the streets of the city filling his stomach with liquor, and pouring out his profanity on God's pure air, and swearing he can whip his weight in wild cats; poor fellow, he is blinded by the devil and led captive at his will. But, bless the Lord, before sundown a severe pain strikes him in the stomach, and in a few minutes his eyes are opened and he sees his awful condition and goes to calling on God for mercy and asking his friends to pray for him. If you had stopped the fellow on the sidewalk and told him God loved him and that you were praying for him, he would have made fun of you to your face, but, thank God, we can never get out of the bow shot of our blessed Heavenly Father, and sometimes the way God can have mercy on us is to let an arrow fly and strike us in the side. How we look up into the face of our loving Father and say, "What is the matter?" and God replies, "If I had not let an arrow fly at you, you would have been in hell in less than a month." Just think of it! if there were no more deathbed scenes, pain or poverty, for the next one hundred years—think of not another

grave dug—no man suffering or seeing his loved ones
die or suffer, to what extent would the whisky element
and the tobacco factories run? Think of the brothels
running day and night without any fear of death or
sickness, with the luxuries of life piled up around
them. Think of how the people of this country would
strut, boast and brag, and curse God to His face, defy
Heaven, burn down churches and make fun of religion.

I tell you, friends, if God did not put on the brakes
it would not be long until the D. Ds. of this country
would have to acknowledge that man was totally depraved, and his heart deceitful above all things and
desperately wicked.

When God gives you a threshing you should be very
thankful, for He will have to beat off the chaff and
burn up the straw before He can gather the wheat
into the garner.

In August, 1902, while at camp meeting at Bonnie,
Ill., in answer to prayer of myself and many friends
the Lord gave my body a retouch and I have been improving every day since. I am able now to preach
once or twice every day and never did better work for
the Lord in my life than I am doing now.

FLASH LIGHTS.

The preacher that comes down out of the sycamore tree and receives the Lord joyfully is a great success.

* * *

The reason your head does not rattle, my friend, is because you have lost the seed out. Do you understand?

* * *

The preacher that can't do anything but turn summersets in the big dipper, shave the man in the moon, and cut off his hair, is a failure.

* * *

I am standing on the promises, walking in His footprints, leaning on His everlasting arms and drinking from the fountain that never runs dry.

* * *

The twin brothers of the Bible: "It shall be done" and "It came to pass," you will find one on every page—one on one page the other one on the other.

* * *

The preacher who is constantly spitting out Greek roots, Latin verbs and Hebrew phrases is seldom ever seen with grape hulls in his beard or the juice on his face.

When I was a sinner God frowned on me; in my justified life He smiled on me; but, in my sanctified life He laughs all over my soul.

* * *

The promises of the Bible are very large; you can lie down and stretch out on them and you can't kick the footboard, scratch the headboard nor touch the railing on either side.

* * *

In looking at the promises of the Bible you think of an apple orchard on a hillside hanging full of ripe fruit; the wind blows them off, they roll down the hill —you have nothing to do but to pick them up and go on eating and praising the Lord.

* * *

A friend came to me not long since and said: "Brother Bud, my religious joy has all leaked out. What is my trouble?" "My!" I said, "my friend, you keep your mouth open all the time." She said, "Thank you, sir," and I said, "You are welcome."

* * *

The Lord said: "The cattle on a thousand hills are mine," and I said, "Yes, Lord, and all the potatoes in the hills." He said: "Buddie, do you want potatoes?" I said, "Yes, Lord." He said, "Go to scratching." I said, "Lord, just watch me scratch," and when He looked at me it almost tickled me to death.

What a sad sight—God's lamb in the devil's cockle-burr patch with his wool full of cockleburrs.

* * *

What is the description of a sanctified man? He has a level head, a sweet spirit, a big soul, a loving disposition and a good heart.

* * *

The religion of Jesus Christ is the principles of God the Father. If you claim it you ought to live as you think He would if he were in your place.

* * *

You can tell a sanctified man anywhere you see him —he has grape hulls in his beard, the juice all over his face and his pockets full of pomegranates.

* * *

The blessing of sanctification doesn't make an A. M. graduate out of a fellow, but it does enable him to make the best use possible of the sense he's got.

* * *

If the Lord is your shepherd, then you are the Lord's sheep, and he has a perfect right to shear you any time he needs wool, and you have no right to bleat.

* * *

Why will a preacher spend his time in staking out claims on Jupiter and Venus, when the Bible describes two other countries and says we are going to one or the other of them?

It is a hopeful sign to see a fellow disgusted with himself but satisfied with Christ.

* * *

God tells us what He wants us to do and He takes it for granted that we ought to believe Him.

* * *

Where is the headquarters of a sanctified man? Why, in the vineyard of the Lord, of course.

* * *

People say the church is dead, and then proceed to . fight a corpse! You look awfully small fighting a corpse.

* * *

If we can fill a man's head full of gospel truth it will soak down into his heart and break out on his face and change his whole life.

* * *

An unsanctified woman is like a bowl of sweet milk —in the morning fresh and sweet, by noon it is blue-john or just a little blinkey, by night sour and clab-bered.

* * *

When I was a sinner I lived on bread and molasses; when I got converted the Lord said, your bread and water shall be sure, and threw in streaked bacon; but since He sanctified me He sets me in a glass cupboard and pitches red apples at me till I laugh myself to sleep.

Common sense religion means to manufacture sunshine and smiles and give them to a lost world.

* * *

The man that it looking into the loving face of Jesus Christ never sees the dark side of life. To him there is but one side, and that is always bright.

* * *

I am often asked by people as I go up and down through the country why a certain young man in the country is not a success. They say he has a fine face and a good education. I tell them it is because he don't succeed well. They say, "Why don't he succeed?" It is because he is a poor sucker.

* * *

The Lord loves to work with people and He loves to have people work with Him. With all the power God has, He don't work by Himself, and the Lord is looking for people that will work with Him, and if you are willing to work with the Lord you will have a companion to work with.

* * *

A young Baptist preacher told me once that bapto and baptizo meant to dip and to plunge. I was a plow-boy and very hungry. I told him if he could show me that gravie, gravi and gravo were the Greek words for good table soup I was a candidate. He just twisted his mustache and went on. You see, I wasn't a Greek scholar.

A man's fortune is made when he reaches the place where he has unloaded carnality and is linked onto God.

* * *

We are all pilgrims, and a pilgrim is a traveler, and every traveler has his companion for life—the Holy Spirit or the evil spirit. My friend, which is yours?

* * *

You can no more wear my religion than you can wear my breeches. It was made for a poor, stuttering Irishman with his elbows out at his shirt sleeves, greasy pants, slouch hat, run-down boots—you don't fill the bill, it wouldn't fit you at all.

* * *

When I was a preacher boy I used to tell my congregation that I was going to preach to their hearts. I thought then their hearts were very soft, but I have now changed my tactics and preach to their heads, for I have found out that men's heads are much softer than their hearts.

* * *

The only way to have the mind of Christ in you is to get rid of the carnal mind, and that is the only trouble you ever had. The trouble you have is not located above your mouth; it is right below your collar bone and a little to the left of your stomach. I could hit you with a biscuit and cover up your trouble.

The man that is satisfied with the world is without God. The man that has God doesn't need the world.

* * *

The reason Christ paid such an enormous price for you, my friend, is because you are to live with Him forever.

* * *

If conversion and sanctification don't keep a man sweet, get him to the altar as quick as possible, and get him to get religion; it will have a wonderful effect on him.

* * *

If the church is dead and I keep on fighting it I prove to the world that I still have faith in it being resurrected, or I prove to the mind of every thinking man that I am diseased just above the ears.

* * *

I am in the Holiness move forever, but let's give the devil his dues. Soured Holiness is the worst form of religion I ever saw, and, my friend, if you are troubled with it, it will kill you if you don't get rid of it.

* * *

The man is a great success that can take the material he has on hand and succeed with it. But you say, "I haven't got anything to start with." Well, who in the world did have? Don't you remember when you were born you had nothing but your little red skin?

It is Christ-like to see something in the other fellow that is better than the things you see in your own self.

* * *

When God sanctifies a preacher He winds him up, sets him on fire and starts him to running, and he has nothing to do but to unwind, shine and shout.

* * *

See that man there squirting tobacco juice out of his mouth? He says he is chewing his cud. Well, hear what Moses says about it: "Any animal that chews his cud that has not got a forked hoof is unclean."

* * *

My friend, if you are troubled with wrinkles on your face, let the Lord wipe His hands on your heart a few times, and when you look at your face you will be surprised, and won't know it, and will wonder where it came from. Why, from Heaven, of course.

* * *

One way of working for the Lord is to pray for the other fellow and love the other fellow, and the only way to do anything for God in this country is to help the other fellow. The only way to reach God is to reach a hand out to the other fellow. If we reach the other fellow we must reach Heaven. And the man that can reach Heaven can reach the other fellow, and the man that can't reach the other fellow can't reach Heaven.

The man that prays louder with a spell of the cramp colic than he does at family prayers would be uneasy at the judgment.

* * *

A good way to get along with the other fellow is to eat bread you can smell perspiration on and you will have the problem about solved. Do you catch on?

* * *

It would be a great business transaction for me to die, for my Heavenly Father has insured me for more than I am worth, and I can only collect the policy by exchanging the cross for my crown. Hallelujah, Amen!

* * *

Four things are needful to understand the Scriptures. 1st. Find out who is doing the talking. 2d. Who he is talking to. 3d. What he is talking about. 4th. Believe he meant just what he said, and the problem is solved.

* * *

If a man gets into a drunken row, and a bartender throws a beer bottle across the bar and knocks one of his eyes out, and in after years we get him converted and sanctified, the blessing of sanctification will not put his eye back, but it will enable him to wake up in the morning of the resurrection with two eyes as bright as twenty-dollar gold pieces.

When a man has gold he is a gold standard man; when he has silver he is a free silver man; when he has greenbacks he is a greenbacker, and when he is broke he is a "pop." Bless the Lord! I am a prohibitioner.

*   *   *

The salvation that Jesus Christ purchased for a lost world is wonderful in its magnitude. It is as deep as fallen humanity, as broad as the compassion of God, as high as Heaven and as everlasting as the eternal Rock of Ages.

*   *   *

What a delusion a man is under! See him in a fit of anger; he thinks he has lost his temper, but you can see he hasn't, for it is hung up all over his face. Anything that is lost is out of sight. Don't you catch on? But he says, "I feel like I have lost something." Well, you have, my brother—it is your religion. Now look into your heart and see.

*   *   *

Christ said: "I will make you fishers of men." Well, thank God! If we tarry for the enduement of power and get our pentecost, pentecostal preaching will catch the fish and clean them after they are caught. The trouble with our churches is in our revivals. We catch and string the fish and don't get them cleaned and they spoil on our hands. You see, it is one thing to catch the fish and another thing to clean them.

Money is the cheapest thing in the world. I suppose it is because it keeps such bad company.

* * *

A physician with eczema on his ankles is never
without a call, and his services are in constant demand
the year round, and he is never without employment.
It is so easy for him to fulfil the Scripture where it
says, "What your hand finds to do, do it with all your
might."

* * *

Did you see that young man on the sidewalk, with
a roll of brown paper in his mouth, one end of it on
fire and something blue coming out of his nose? Yes!
What in the world is his trouble? Why, he has bad
thoughts, bad dreams and bad conduct, and he is trying
to purify his brains. It is generally supposed he has
the hollow head. Oh, my! What a disease!

* * *

I said to my congregation one morning: "My
friends, I am glad to inform you that I have at last
located your trouble. It is just below your collar bone
and a little to the left of your stomach." A man spoke
up and said: "Is it heart failure?" I said, "Oh, no.
When you see a man gritting his teeth, slamming doors,
knocking down chairs and pulling his hair, you know
his heart hasn't failed. He is suffering with carnality."

Oh, this great salvation! It justifies freely, sanctifies wholly, cleanses thoroughly and keeps sweetly.

* * *

Somehow you always associate money and politics together. They are sort o' like the sun and moon—one rules by day and the other by night.

* * *

The first debt I owe this country is a good man; the second, a good husband; the third, a good father; the fourth, a good neighbor, and if God will furnish the grace I will furnish the man. "For ye are workers together with Him." See the Bible.

* * *

If a man's mind is located in his head, then some men's heads are nothing but a garbage box, and their mouth a second-class sewerage. How disgusting he is. When you meet with such a fellow you feel like you needed a good bath and a few hours' sleep.

* * *

But you say there is nobody that can live where you live and live a sanctified life. Well, I believe it, because you are living in the kingdom of sin. Move over into the kingdom of grace and you will talk differently. But you say, "I never saw one that lived it." Well, my neighbor, that proves that you have been keeping awfully bad company. If you will change crowds you will see things quite differently.

See the man coming down the street sucking at the end of an old pipe stem?—you can smell him fifty yards. As he goes by I think of the words of a young woman who said, "Lord, by this time he stinketh."

* * *

The man that has God for his Father, and Jesus Christ for his Saviour, the Holy Ghost for his abiding comforter and the redeemed saints of all the ages for his brothers and sisters, the angels for his companions and Heaven for his eternal home, thank God, his fortune is made.

* * *

The man that is a stockholder in the clouds surely walks on earth and lives in Heaven. Did you hear what Paul said about it? He said, "For our conversation is in Heaven from whence we look for the Saviour the Lord Jesus Christ." Don't you see if your conversation is in Heaven you must live there?

* * *

The difference between us and the Lord is, the Lord came to see us and we made Him pay His tax—we went to see Him and He paid ours. Bless His dear name! See the difference? The sinner doesn't serve God at all. The regenerated man serves God through a sense of duty. The sanctified man serves God through a sense of love. Which crowd are you running with, my friend?

This great salvation is knowable, feelable, enjoyable, livable, but not explainable.

* * *

"The leaves of the tree were for the healing of the nations." The finest salad in the world beats turnip greens.

* * *

To endure to the end doesn't mean to endure your religion. You endure a corn on your toe or a carbuncle on your neck.

* * *

The blessing of sanctification will not keep you from snoring in your sleep, but, bless the Lord, it will cause you to wake up in a good humor.

* * *

There are 66 books in the Bible, 1,189 chapters, 31,-173 verses, 773,746 words, 3,566,480 letters, and every book, chapter, verse, word and letter is an index finger pointing to the Christ of Prophecy, the Christ of Bethlehem, the Christ of Calvary, and, thank God, the Christ that walked off from Mt. Olivet on the clouds saying, "Goodbye, boys; I am going to prepare a place for you, and if I go and prepare a place for you I will come again and receive you unto Myself, that where I am there ye may be also." Do you wonder they stood looking up into the clouds? Why, praise the Lord, no!

If thick milk is clabber, then your cow is a clabber sprout, and when you milk your cow, properly speaking, you are juicing your clabber sprout.

* * *

The way to make a success of life when you meet with a disappointment is just drop the letter "d" and put "h" instead, and then see what it spells—H-I-S-A-P-P-O-I-N-T-M-E-N-T. Well, Bless the Lord! Don't you see that puts you in regular succession?

* * *

I have seen cows with tongues long enough to lick their calves through the crack of the fence. "Well," you say, "that is a mighty long tongue." Yes, but I have seen longer tongues than that. I have seen people that could sit in their own parlor and lick their neighbors all around the country. They would make you think of a wagon—they need a breast-yoke to hold their tongue up.

* * *

That old adage, "If at first you don't succeed, try, try again," I never did like, for the way to succeed is to suck 'till you get the seed. Hear St. John on this seed business: "For whosoever is born of God doth not commit sin, for His seed remaineth in him and he cannot sin because he is born of God." You see, God furnishes the seed and you have nothing to do but suck. Well, Glory! Isn't that fine?

* * *

The reason why I had rather be a dog than a mean white man: The dog licks his own mouth, but a mean man licks his wife.

* * *

The man is a great success in this life that can gather up sunshine all day and spread it out on the fly leaves of his brain pan, and come in at night, unfold the leaves and show it to his wife and babies.

* * *

The religion that is full of juice is full of teeth, and a religion with teeth in it will bite, and if it bites it will get hold of somebody and they will holler, and when a fellow hollers you have him located and you know where to work.

* * *

There is such a hollow sound about what a fellow says when he keeps his head open all the time. It sounds a great deal like a boy beating on a barrel with the bunghole open. Why don't he bring his tongue in out of the weather and shut his mouth?

* * *

The most disgusting thing I ever saw was a man standing on a street corner, with bloodshot eyes, a red nose, a bloated face, and a big stomach on him, sucking at an old pipe, with the smell of strong drink on his breath, and dirty clothes on his body, talking about the "Mistakes of Moses" and the "Failures of Christianity."

The way to get along well with your neighbor is to keep the rat hole in your noggin closed.

* * *

Success and succeed are twin brothers and are the sons of Industry and Determination, and they have never made a failure politically, socially, financially, mentally or spiritually.

* * *

We are printing 10,000,000 copies of the Bible annually in 325 different languages. If one Bible is 10 inches long the 10,000,000 copies are 1,574 1-4 miles long. Set them on edge and they would make a fence 8 inches high; throw into a square and you have a pasture of nearly 400 miles square.

* * *

Some people say they can't stand Bud Robinson. Well, I'm not good-looking nor brainy, but if you don't love me the devil will get you.

* * *

There are many different ways of getting an income; mine comes through my mouth and goes the same way. A man's mouth is a fortune or a misfortune, owing to the use you put it to and who you use it for. A clean mouth, consecrated to God, may bless the world a hundred years after you are dead. God said, Open thy mouth wide and I will fill it.

An abundant entrance doesn't mean hubbing the gate post on each side or escaping hell by the skin of the teeth.

*   *   *

I know of nothing that brings greater joy to my heart than to know that God will trust me as far as I trust Him. If I trust Him clear up to Heaven He will trust me clear down to earth. If I will trust Him all over Heaven He will trust me all over the earth. When we trust each other we rely on and confide in each other. How blessed the fellowship.

*   *   *

It takes less religion to criticise than anything else in the world. I have tried it, and when a fellow tries and proves anything he knows what he is talking about.

*   *   *

I have met so many people in my travels who told me they hated their neighbor's ways awfully bad, but loved his soul. I always feel a little bit uneasy about him. I am persuaded if you will boil down your hatred, skim it and analyze the skimmings you will find you hate the whole fellow, and John said: "If any man hate his brother he is a murderer," and we know that no murderer has eternal life abiding in him, and, friend, if you are hating a fellow's ways it would not be a bad idea for you to go to the mourners' bench and at least take an inventory of your stock of goods.

You can't draw on the bank for what you used to have. You can only check out what you have in it now.

* * *

How easy it is for God to pardon a poor boy who has stolen bread and meat. But a theological rascal who undermines the religion of his flock is the worst kind of a thief in the sight of God. I believe preachers are the best sort of men in the world when they are good. But they are the worst sort of men in the world when they are bad.

* * *

I have heard people say, "I believe in Holiness, but I don't believe in sanctification." They are like the old woman who loved mutton, but couldn't eat sheep. She felt like she was getting wool in her teeth.

* * *

The fellow that says he is sanctified will have no trouble in establishing the fact if he can show the fruit. To illustrate: An Irishman was on trial in one of our county courts. The county judge said to him: "Are you a married man?" The Irishman never opened his mouth, but proceeded to take off his hat, and showed a scar on the side of his head that looked something like a fire shovel. The judge said: "I accept the evidence; you may stand aside." He showed the fruit.

I have had folks make fun of me for not using good grammar, when the only way they had their name in the county paper was when their father had paid them out of a scrape. I've had, at times, preachers make fun of my English, when the only tears shed under their ministry were the tears of babies crying for water. My brother, if I were you and couldn't tree a 'possum I wouldn't kill the dog who did.

* * *

The young woman that knows how to pray, run a sewing machine, cook stove, washboard, flatiron and milk the cow, never jumps head-first into the river, because she has an easy conscience and a light heart, and with a smile on her face she goes on turning everything she touches into sunshine.

But the young woman that can't do anything but look pretty, wear fine clothes, put on perfumery and dead birds and flirt with a little fellow blowing blue smoke out of his nose and driving a livery rig, soon becomes disgusted with the world and worse with herself; life becomes a burden and a drag. She decides to end her miserable existence by jumping head-first into the river. She is dragged out the second day, buried the third, and by the fourth she is forgotten, because she did nothing to bless the world while she lived in it.

The beauty of Jesus Christ was that He saw something all the time in man that was worth dying for.

* * *

You notice around depots, hotels and many public places, "No loafing allowed here." Who ever saw that sign on an undertaker's establishment. Ye upper and lower tens dread the black box and a hole in the ground at the end of your life, for "It is appointed unto man once to die, but after this the Judgment."

* * *

"Equal rights to all men and special rights to none." Christ knocks at my door here and I knock at His door over there. If I open to Him here He will open to me there. Isn't that fair?

* * *

The first president of the First Holiness Association was Job. His three friends started for Job's Holiness Meeting. They brought their bullocks and rams, as the Lord commanded them, for a burnt offering. They inquired at every cross road the way to Job's Holiness Meeting. They were opposed to the Holiness Convention, but went with their offerings, and they had to pay the expense of the meeting. The last we heard of them Job had them at the altar praying for them, beating them on the back and shouting, and asking them if they had the blessing.

You need to belong to the Aid Society. You are needing help.

* * *

Well, Glory to God! In conversation with the dear Lord this morning, I said: "Lord, where must I get to keep from falling?" "Why," He said, "my son, get on the bottom." Well, Glory. "Can't a preacher fall from the bottom?" "No." The Lord said, "There is no place below the bottom." Well, Hallelujah! I looked around and to my surprise I found that the home of my blessed Christ was at the bottom.

* * *

People talk to me of their good blood; about their Cousin William, who was a merchant, doctor or lawyer. Why don't you talk about your Cousin John some? He likely is in the pen for killing a negro.

* * *

A sanctified man has a shining face, an easy conscience, and a light heart, and is as bold as a lion, as patient as an ox, as swift as an eagle, as wise as a serpent, as harmless as a dove, as gentle as a lamb, and as sweet as honey. If you were to slap his jaws you would get honey all over your hand, and as you walked away you would feel something sticky on your hand. Lick it off and get under conviction, and come back to see what ailed him, and find out it was perfect love.

When this old world is wrapped in a winding sheet of flames you will forget the "mistakes of Moses" and be brought face to face with your own mistakes and misconduct.

* * *

If you blaze every tree, tunnel a hole through every mountain, make a bridge over every river, it looks like I could find the way and wouldn't just quit the road and go out into the woods. Well, my friends, the Bible is plainer than that, and it looks like you could find the way to Heaven.

* * *

So many people have told me the churches are all dead, but I can't believe it; for as long as an institution can play cards, fry oysters or get up a broom drill they surely have some evidences of life, and as long "As the lamp holds out to burn the vilest sinner may return."

* * *

The Lord wants all my sins. He said He would bury them in the depths of the sea. Then he said, "Perhaps Buddie will go diving some day and find them," so He said: "I will separate them from him as far as the east is from the west." Then He said: "He may fly over there when he gets his golden wings," so He said, "I'll beat that, Buddie, I'll blot them out of the book of remembrance forever."

Sanctification is free. You have to give yourself for it, but you are nothing and you give yourself (nothing) for it. God takes what you think you are and gives you sanctification.

* * *

Two of the most unnatural looking things in the world: One is a backslidden preacher; the other is a long-tailed mule. The mule needs shearing, and the preacher has been sheared. See the Bible: "And while he slept, with his head on her lap, they sheared off his locks."

* * *

My friend, if you are making a bee line for the New Jerusalem, the greatest accusation that will be brought against you at the judgment will be that you saw something in every human being worth dying for.

* * *

Two of the greatest enemies of my life have been the carnal mind and my mouth. The carnal mind would get up at the wrong time and my mouth would go off at the wrong time. If I could have kept a watch on my mouth it would have saved me so much trouble. If there was a law passed to cut the end off the tongues of everybody in this country that has said an unkind word about his neighbor, you would see this fellow packing his grip. This land would make you think of the confusion of tongues at the Tower of Babel.

I had rather be a poor rich man than a rich poor man. A poor rich man has no money, but plenty of salvation. A rich poor man has plenty of money but no grace.

* * *

The fellow that lets his religion all go out but a "spark" is in a "strait betwixt two." He has too much to throw away and not enough to keep. If he stays and blows the spark he can't do anything else, and if he runs to get kindling it will go out on him.

* * *

The Holy Ghost is God's officer in the world, trying to arrest the sinner and bring him to Jesus Christ, who is the judge of the quick and dead, and the judge will pardon every sinner that will yield to the officer and come to Him for trial.

* * *

St. Paul was greatly troubled with a fellow he called "Alexander the Coppersmith." I see some marks of similarity between Paul and myself. I have been bothered with that same fellow. I notice he is still a great drawback to the churches. When I see the collectors coming back with only a few pennies in the hat, I know Alex. is on hand. When a man puts in a copper when he should put in 5, 10, 25 or 50 cents, he is an Alexander Coppersmith. Alex. has a mighty following today.

A religion that won't keep you sweet when the cow and calf get together, or the old sow eats up the chickens, won't be worth paying taxes on when this old world gets on fire.

*   *   *

One of the greatest needs of the Holiness movement is more hands to put on plasters and fewer hands to skin. Human hides are awful cheap now. It may be because money is so scarce. I am not sure about that, as there has not been a great demand for human hides for the last two or three centuries.

*   *   *

I have seen young women come to the altar chewing gum and fanning themselves with a little silk fan and say, "I don't care anything about it myself, Brother Bud. If the Lord wants to save me I'm willing." My! my! Sister, your head is clabber on both sides.

*   *   *

Now, the object of a plaster is to draw. You remember Christ said: "If I be lifted up I will draw all men unto me." Brother, you shake up your head a little and see if you can see any difference between skinning and drawing. I have seen the hardest sinners of the land stand in the hot sun for several hours to hear about the Man that wore the seamless coat, while you can't keep a crowd thirty minutes to hear about hoofs and horns. Do you see any difference?

My brother, if they tell you to give up your conscience or give up your church—as you have only one conscience and there are many churches—just pack your grip, call your dog and start and keep going until the Lord stops you.   *   *   *

How many little flirts I have seen go to a little dance (a kind of a hugging school), come home at the break of day looking like a greasy dish rag, rub off the prepared chalk and paint, take off the false curls and want to commit suicide.

*   *   *

I dreamed one night of going to Heaven and eating fruit off of the tree of life as big as my two fists without any peeling on it or seed in it. It was so good it melted in my mouth. I couldn't eat Texas grub hardly for a month after I woke.

*   *   *

The devil said to me one day, "The Lord is not able to do what you ask." I just turned to my Bible and read: "Who hath measured the waters in the hollow of His hand and meted out Heaven with a span and comprehended the dust of the earth in a measure and weighed the mountains and the hills in a balance." Had you considered the greatness of God and His ability to meet our necessities? I asked. He sneaked away and wasn't hanging around my premises again for a week.

The difference between a preacher and a county judge is this: The preacher adds one to one and the sum is one; the judge subtracts one from one and the sum is two. We beat them in grace but they are ahead of us in mathematics.

* * *

When our blessed Saviour was on earth He worked a miracle to raise money to pay His taxes. Well, bless His dear name, He has been working miracles to pay mine for the last twenty years. Don't you know I love Him? Of course I do!

* * *

It matters not how many business houses close or how many men are thrown out of work, there is one class of people who are never without a job—that is the faultfinder and the chronic grumbler. They have a job the year round, and they stick to their bush.

SAYINGS AND SERMONS.

COMMON SENSE.

The religion of Jesus Christ is just good common sense, that's all. If you have got it you're a sensible man, that's all. If you haven't got it, you haven't got good common sense, that's all.—(Prov. 1:7.) If you haven't got it, you are on the road to hell—that's all.

THE GRACE OF GOD.

There is something very peculiar about the grace of God. When a man gets under conviction it is up to his ankles, when he repents it is knee deep, when he exercises a living faith it is up to his loins, when he is converted it is over his head, when he is sanctified he has grace to swim in, and when he is glorified he goes to flying. Well, Glory! Isn't it grand?

MAKING BOOKS.

The reason why it is so difficult to make a book is that the maker is required to spread his brains out on paper. The reader will see at once that this is indeed a difficult task. In the first place you have got to have the brains, in the second place you have got to spread them out, and last, but not least, you may not have

them to spare, as times have been a little dull and there
has been quite a demand for the article of late.

GOD'S X RAYS.

"For the Word of God is quick and powerful and
sharper than a two-edged sword, piercing even to the
dividing asunder of soul and spirit and of the joints
·and marrow and is a discerner of the thoughts and
intents of the heart.

"Neither is there any creature that is not manifest
in his sight, but all things are naked and open unto
the eyes of him with whom we have to do."—Hebrews
4:12, 13.

SILENCED BY HIS OWN ARGUMENT.

I heard a man one day butcher up to his neighbors.
I sat and meditated as he paraded their faults and weaknesses before me. The next day the same man heard me
preach. He came up with a big grin all over his face
and said, "Bro. Bud, you surely butcher up the English
language, old boy." I said, "Yes, that's what people tell
on me, but it is so much easier on a man's conscience to
butcher up the English language than to butcher up his
neighbor." And he was like "a sheep before her shear-
ers—dumb, so he opened not his mouth."

A Dead Religion.

A juiceless religion is toothless, lifeless, powerless, and dead. A dead religion was hatched out of the old nest egg from under the mudsill of perdition, and was one of the first broods that Splitfoot hatched off. I don't know how long he set on the nest, but I am sure he hatched every egg he set on. A dead religion has cursed the church, wrecked the faith and blasted the hopes of multiplied millions of the sons and daughters of Adam.

The Difference Between Two Women.

When you see a woman full of sin, fashion, pride and the devil, the first thought that comes to your mind is, "Has she got a pretty face?" But when you meet with a woman with clean hands and a pure heart, who hath not lifted up her soul to vanity, nor sworn deceitfully, you never think of her face, but look at the beautiful life, and as she goes by you take off your hat and put it under your arm and feel like you are standing on holy ground.

Patching a Broken Heart with Calico.

I have known a man to say things to his wife that almost broke her heart, and not have manhood enough to apologize to her. A week after he goes to town and gets her a cheap calico dress—only paying a nickel a yard for it—brings it home and throws it down in her lap. He is trying to patch up a broken heart with calico. Friend, it won't work that way. You can't heal a wound with dry goods. It isn't calico that a woman wants—it's a *husband*.

A Poor Threshing Machine.

I have seen churches where they paid the preacher, got up conference collections, sent out missionary money, run an Epworth League, helped the Christian Endeavor and Young Men's Christian Association, yet lost members every year.

Now, friend, don't you know if I was running a threshing machine, cooking for the hands, feeding the mules, raising a dust and burning the straw, and were to go around and look at the spout and find no wheat coming out, it would be common sense in me to quit.

In the World but not of the World.

Christ said he was in the world and the world was made by him, and the world knew him not. He also taught that his followers are to be in the world and yet not of the world, for he said, "I have taken you out of the world, for the world will love its own and them only." So you see, friend, if you keep out of the world you will get into heaven and if you keep out of heaven you will get into hell, so our only hope is to take the scriptural route. In regeneration God takes us out of the world; in sanctification he takes the world out of us.

SAUL OF TARSUS.

When the Lord wanted to make an impression on this old world that men or devils, time or eternity could not erase, he met Saul of Tarsus on the Damascus road and pulled him off of his little donkey and put him to praying. Three days later he shook the scales from off his eyes, charged him with compound lightning, wound him up and put him to running. The Lord seemed to take him in his own hand, dip him in the blood of Jesus Christ and write across the face of the earth: "Follow peace with all men, and holiness, without which no man shall see the Lord."

FLAT AND LEVEL.

What strange critters we mortals be. Strange indeed; yes, indeed; if you tell a fellow that his head is perfectly level, smiles and sunshine will play up and down on his face like sun perch and speckled trout in a springing brook in the month of June, and he will give you a hearty handshake and say "Luck to you, old boy," and will give you one of his photos to remem-

ber him by; but if you tell him his head is perfectly
flat, anger will crawl over his face like worms on the
tobacco leaves and he will give you a licking to remember him by.   See the difference between flat and level.

GIFTS AND GRACES—THE CARNAL MIND.

The gifts and graces of the spirit and the weaknesses
of the carnal mind are not twin brothers, as you might
suppose.   In fact they are no kin at all; not even third
cousins, for while the gifts and graces seem to be frag-
rant with grapes, pomegranates and flowers, freighted
with the mountains, lakes and rainbows of Heaven, red
white and golden clouds, dews and showers of glory,
the carnal mind seems to be perfumed with tobacco,
alcohol, smoke and sulphur, filthy conversation and talking, you can see a few hoofs and horns and broken bones
scattered along the public highway.

A CHURCH ENTERTAINMENT.

I suppose Moses left about as spiritual a congregation
as most preachers, when he went on Mt. Sinai and was
gone only about forty days, and to his surprise when he
got back in hearing of the multitude, they had forsaken
God and gone after a calf, and, worse still, it was a
home-made calf.   You see Aaron's calf was a kind of
church entertainment affair.   The first one, I suppose,

the boys ever got up. The object of the calf show was to take the place of God and the Holy Ghost. This church entertainment was a failure, as all its successors have been, and ended in raising a dust and breaking the ten commandments.

A Hypocrite Not In A Christian's Way.

To say there are no hypocrites in the church would be false; to say they are in my way would be equally false, for a Christian and a hypocrite are not on the same road; not traveling in the same direction, and of course could not be in each other's way. The only way a fellow can be in my way is for him to be ahead of me, and for me to confess that hypocrites and sinners are in my way! My! I will never do it in the world. Don't you know if you stumble over a fellow he is ahead of you? You never stumble over an object behind you.

When You Pray.

My friend, when you pray if nobody talks back to you it would be well for you to stop long enough to find out how you stand at headquarters. It may be possible your name has been dropped from the ledger, and if so you will never get another answer until you are represented by the man with the seamless coat on, with blood and spittle on his face and the print of nails in his feet and hands and a spear print in his side and a crown of thorns on his head, and when the Father looks into the face of this mangled victim for sin, if he is pleading for you, the great loving heart of the Father will be moved with compassion toward you and he will talk with you on any subject and not only that, but glory to God, he will give you anything he has got.

WHY ?

Why will a preacher go into the pulpit on Sunday morning and read an essay on Socrates, Cicero or the Queen of England, when he knows it is as dry as a Texas wind and as empty as a last years' bird's nest? He knows it won't convict sinners, convert mourners, sanctify believers or build up the church. Such preaching never makes a man cry, laugh, get mad or shout. In fact, it won't even keep his congregation awake. While he turns the pages of his manuscript many in his congregation have moved to the land of Nod, and the official board have consulted napper two or three times and report everything running smoothly, no excitement, wild-fire, or fanaticism, but the church in a prosperous condition and a bright outlook for the future.

A Point On Total Depravity.

An old lady in the mountains of Tennessee was fixing one morning to go and spend the day with a sick neighbor, and before leaving home she called up the children, and said, "Your mother has to go to wait on a sick woman today and I'll not get back till night, and if you children go up stairs and look in the old chest and get out my pumpkin seeds and eat them up, and if you look up over the east window and take down my poke of striped seed beans and cram your noses full, when I come back here tonight I will beat your heads till they are as soft as pumpkins." She got on her old pacing pony and went down the road raising the dust. It will suffce to say, that when she came in that night every pumpkin seed had been eaten up and every bean had been planted deep in the noggins of those mountain boys. Shame on the man that denies total depravity.

Denying Total Depravity.

If we were not totally depraved, why would we be ashamed of a small head, a big foot, or a wart on the nose? The majority of the people of today are wearing shoes at least two numbers too small for them. The most of us are ashamed to go into a business house and call for a pair of shoes large enough. They tell us that the Chinese women put their babies' feet into an iron shoe, and we send ten cents to China to enlighten the heathen and spend twenty-five cents at home for corn medicine. We send missionaries to teach them not to drown their baby girls, while we enlightened, educated Christians of America destroy our children before they are born. Oh, my friend! which side of the creek is the heathen on? If we were straight up and right down, and up right, down right, in right, out right and all right we would not be ashamed of anything but sin. The man that denies total depravity shows that "the trail of the serpent" is over him still.

The River of Death.

As a people we have done many exploits. We have bridged the rivers, belted the mighty deep with our ocean liners, tunneled through the great mountains, harnessed the lightning and put it to work, but just ahead of you, my friend, is a little stream without a bridge or steamer. You can't swim across it, but will have to wade through it. It is so cold it will freeze you to death. It is so dark you can't see your way. When you reach the banks of this stream you may see a torchlight procession, shining faces and hear sweet music on the other side. If so, it will have a wonderful effect upon the chilly waters as you wade through, but reader, it may be possible that when you reach that stream you may hear wails and shrieks of the lost and hear the victorious shouts of devils as they drag their victims through the muddy waters of this awful river of death. "Now is the accepted time; behold, now is the day of salvation."—2d Cor. 6:12.

LIKE SHEPHERD, LIKE SHEEP.

When a preacher says a great deal about loyalty to the church, his members say but little about holiness to the Lord. If he is a tobacco chewer, his members seldom go to class meeting; if he is a smoker, they never shout; if he goes to the theater, they go to the ball room, the circus, card table and wine suppers. You see the shepherd feeds the flock, and when you see the sheep you can tell what the shepherd has been feeding them on. No use to consult the shepherd. If the sheep are poor and sickly and their wool full of cockleburrs and Spanish needles, you can tell at a glance just the kind of pasture the sheep have been grazed on. No use to waste time going to look at the pasture; just get a good look at the sheep, and it sufficeth us. Now, reader, notice the shepherd at the annual conference. He comes in with a grass sack full of wool and reports a glorious outlook for the church in the future. 'Tis in the future. If God will furnish a man elbow grease and create for him a mule, he surely ought to do the plowing.

NOT PLACE BUT CONDITION.

The most people seem to think they have the worst neighbors in the world, and think they could be very happy if they only lived somewhere else; but, my friend, that is a mistake. The trouble is not always with the other fellow. It is not the *place* you are in that makes you happy, but the *condition* that you are in. It is not what your neighbors say about you; it is what God knows you to be. If you stand well at headquarters, you can get down on your knees by your fireside and shake hands with the Lord. Glory to God! And of course you can shake hands with every neighbor you have, and rivers of salvation will run down out of the clouds and break in on your soul, and you will love God with a perfect heart and your neighbor as yourself. And then, my brother, you won't want to move, for you will have the best neighbors in the world, and you just can't afford to leave them. But you say, "Brother Bud, how do you know that?" Well, I know it because I have tried it.

A CAMP MEETING SCENE.

It is wonderful how the Lord at times and under some circumstances can use such peculiar means to bless his people. I remember one morning, on one of our leading camp grounds of Texas, we were having a testimony meeting. A man got up and told a long, dry experience, and as he sat down the thought came into my mind, and I said, "My friends, that is a Texas long-horn." As I said it a little woman jumped up and told a red-hot experience full of juice and fire, with a shining face and her little hand raised to heaven. The Spirit seemed to fill me and I jumped up on the platform and said, "Glory to God, that is a short-horn." As I looked at the great congregation I said, "This woman did not give us a herd of cattle, but a pitcher of cream," and it seemed the Spirit swept down in great waves and rolled over the people till they leaped, shout-ed, jumped benches and hugged each other. Sinners wept aloud and ran to the altar, and it seemed to us that rivers of full salvation were rolling over the camp ground. A big fellow jumped up on a bench and said, "Where did you get that?" I said, "From the Lord, I guess, for I never had it before."

An All-'round Man.

An all-'round man has two legs, two arms, two eyes, two ears, one mouth and one nose. His head is his upper end; his feet his lower end. He comes to this country without being sent after. This country is under no obligations to him. He comes here as an intruder. The country has a right to expect great things of him.

He has no right to expect anything of this country and all he gets is gratis. He is expected to wear breeches every day and to go barefooted every night. He should be a good citizen, a good neighbor, a good and loving husband, and further, he should be a man of good common sense, with a shining face and a grand appetite. He should have a kind word, a smile and a hand-shake for every fellow he meets. He should lie down eight hours, stand up eight hours and sit down eight hours out of every twenty-four in the year. The church and state have a right to demand his support; he should serve both cheerfully. He should be a Christian worker and a man of faith and great piety. He should believe the Bible, love God, serve him and his country, walking in the light, leaning on the everlasting arms, drinking from the fountain that never runs dry and go to heaven in the end.

Nervousness and Positiveness.

When a religious woman loses her temper, slams the doors, kicks the chairs over and slaps her baby boy on the side of the head and says to him, "You little rascal, you are just like that old daddy of yours," as the baby goes around the corner of the table snubbing, she says, "You would provoke the angels; you have aggravated your mother this morning until I am so nervous I can't control myself." You see, she calls it nervousness, when the long and short of it was, the old lion just got up and shook himself, and of course he shook the woman, too.—See Isaiah 35:8-9-10. Her husband, who is a pillar of the church and a member of the official board, gets mad and does and says things that a respectable sinner ought not to do. He calls it positiveness, and says, "I always was of a very positive make-up; my neighbors and friends never did understand me." Well, the reason we don't understand you, my brother, is because you claim to be a Christian and live like a sinner. If you will bring your life up to your profession it will be no trouble for you to make your neighbors understand you. The Bible says, "Ye shall know them by their fruit." It is a fearful thing to see a man and his wife controlled by the carnal mind, one calling it nervousness and the other calling it positiveness. What will their children call it?

ADAM THE FIRST.

Adam was not born like the rest of us folks. He was created out of the dust of the earth about January 6th, in the year one. He was not a Seventh Day Adventist, for the Lord made him late Saturday evening. The next day was Sunday, and of course the first day Adam ever saw. The Lord rested that day from his work.

Adam had not done anything and was not tired, but
he kept the first day with the Lord. You see it was
the seventh day with the Lord; but Eve was probably
made about January 8th in the same year with Adam.
It is likely when Adam woke up on Monday morning
he found Eve there. The book says she was made out
of one of Adam's ribs. It has always seemed that
woman had finer material in her than man. I suppose
it is because man was made out of the dust of the earth
and woman out of a man's rib. Doubtless Adam and
Eve loved at sight. Well, why not? Who ever saw
a fellow who did not love his own bones. Adam can
truthfully say he was the first man on earth who lost
a bone.

I suppose Adam and Eve started out in life with the
finest prospects before them of any young couple that
ever started out in this world, but like many folks nowadays, they did not run long until they collapsed. They
sinned against God and lost their beautiful home in
Eden. The Lord sent them out to till the ground.
Adam had no idea that he was the first farmer on earth,
but as he went to tilling the ground he felt like he was
scratching his mother's head and to his surprise at
every scratch he found a piece of bread, and as he
plowed through the field Mother Earth looked on her
first son and smiled and said: "My son is making his
mark in the world."

RELIGION LIKE GOOD BREAD.

Religion is like good bread. To make good biscuit, put in a little salt and soda and lard and sour milk; then make up your biscuit and put them into a stove pan, put them in the stove to bake and they rise; then take them out of the stove a-smoking, with brown backs and white hearts, and, breaking them open, put a little Jersey butter on them, and, with the first bite, you make a new moon out of it, and it is so good that with the second bite there is a total eclipse.

AN INFIDEL'S ATTACK.

When I was in New England an infidel attacked me for preaching that there was a hell. He told me Lyman Abbott had proved there was no hell. I said to him: "Now, my friend, who on earth did he prove that by? He didn't prove it by me; he never even consulted me about it." He looked at me perfectly surprised and said: "Are you the cowboy preacher from Texas?" I said: "Yes, I came from Texas and I have seen cows out there." He said: "We don't need such preachers as you here. You ought to go to Chicago. Don't you know we have the brainiest men and women in the world here? I can produce fifty thousand of the brainiest men and women of the City of Boston of my faith." I said to him: "Yes, you have more brains and less manhood than any gang I ever saw—fifty thousand of you going in a solid platoon to a yawning, gaping, burning hell, where the devil will pour salty damnation down you. He will set you in a corner for a slop tub. You will be a laughing stock for the devil and his imps throughout an endless eternity." He answered: "Why, young man, if you could convince me there was a hell I would cancel my engagements to lecture against Christianity." I said: "My brother, I can't convince you. The Bible says, 'The fool hath said in his heart there is no God.' The probabilities are that you will never get your eyes open until, like the rich man the Scripture mentions, you lift up your eyes in hell, being in torment, and you will want to send missionaries back to preach to your Bostonians, but God won't let you."

GET RID OF SELF, SHOW CHRIST.

How unselfish the Father, Son and Holy Ghost; neither of them ever refer to themselves. How different from we fallen mortals. When we do anything it is I, we or us. When God the Father came to us he spoke of the law; when Christ came he spoke of the Father; when the Holy Ghost came he spoke of the Son. When we get converted we talk about going to heaven; when we get sanctified we talk about the blessed Holy Ghost, for we then have heaven in us, the Holy Ghost revealing to us the law as our school master bringing us to Christ. He reveals to us God as our Father; he reveals Christ as our blessed Savior and Sanctifier, and himself as our abiding guest. He makes the Fatherhood of God and the brotherhood of man so plain that not one doubt remains in the heart to disturb your peace. But he enables you to love God with all your heart and your neighbor as yourself, for the perfect love of God will cast out all fear and doubt and selfishness and make you like Jesus Christ, the most unselfish being that ever lived on the earth. So then if you want to show Christ to this old world you will have to get rid of self, for as long as there is any self in you the world can't see Jesus Christ. Remember, friend, the world don't read their Bible. They read you, and when you buy beefsteak the butcher is to feel like he is selling meat to one of God's sons. And now sister, what about that hat you bought. Do you suppose the woman who sold you that hat felt like she was selling one of God's daughters a hat? Did you act in a way to convince her that Jesus Christ lived in your home? Now the Book says we are sons and daughters of the Lord Almighty, and if we don't show our Heavenly Father to the world as we buy and sell, under what circumstances then are we to show Him to the world.

WHAT COMMON FOLKS DON'T KNOW.

There are so many things we common people don't know, and in fact never heard of, that we surely ought to keep our heads open. We see a great college president going down the streets of our cities on a beautiful automobile and we notice a little platform on a street corner, and a monkey with red breeches on it cutting monkey shines, while the boys give him sugar. We see the president slow up his automobile and his great heart seems to warm up to the monkey. He takes out his family record and shows us the very year that his folks and the monkey's family lived in the same hollow log. I tell you it makes us country boys scratch our heads. Presently the president pulls the lever of his automobile and goes up the street at the rate of thirty miles an hour and presently he slows up again and we notice on the corner a Turkish boy and a cinnamon bear wrestling together, and every time the bear throws the boy it nearly tickles the president to death, and he says, "We are still ahead." Again he takes out his family record and can show you the exact year that his great-great-great-grandfather was united in holy wedlock to Miss Cinnamon Bear. As the little Turk leads the bear away the president smiles and says: "Now, just look at me and see what a wonderful improvement we have made on our family." We country boys just grin and say what a pity we uneducated people have lost our family record. We go on up the street a little farther, we meet a rich woman driving down the street in a beautiful carriage, with diamonds flashing from her ears, gold bands on her fingers and arms. She is embracing a poodle dog. We say: "Well, I guess she has met one of her cousins"—for everybody knows that a woman has a perfect right to hug her kinfolks—and we country folks just make up our minds that we are not in the thing at all.

THE BREAKING OF DAY.

The man that loves God with all his heart, soul and mind and strength, and his neighbor as himself, and his family better than himself, can walk on the earth all day with an easy conscience and a contented mind, and lie down at night and go to sleep, feeling that the wings of angels are spread out over him. He will wake up in the morning and look out over the eastern horizon and see the sun roll up from behind its eastern hills and wash his hands in the blue skies and wipe them off on the clouds of heaven. As he wipes his face you can see scarlet all over the clouds, and as he wipes his hands you can see long finger prints of orange all over the clouds, and he seems to step to the rack and hang up the towel. As you watch the towel a moment you see the scarlet and orange smiling on each other, and the fellow says: "Well, well, the angels are having ice cream for breakfast." An angel whispers to him and says: "No, friend, the sun is just washing his face, that is all." As you take your eyes off of the towel and look at the sun, he seems to step to the portico and throw out his wash water, and it comes splashing and sprinkling down over the hillsides of earth, covering the grass with dew drops to shine and glitter and sparkle in the eyes of the early riser. It rolls on down the hillside until all the hollow places and valleys are full of sunshine, and the fellow looks out of his window and sees the last little piece of darkness flying across the mountain top chased by a thousand sunbeams. He hears the mocking bird sing in the elm, and the joree in the hackberry, the cackling of fowls in the barnyard and the cooing of the dove on the yard fence. "Well, day has broken," says the man who is rising. "Oh, no," the sun says, "my friend, you cannot break the day, for it is God's face turned toward the earth; but we have just broken the night loose from the earth. Didn't you see the last piece of it going across the mountains?"

The Devil's Truck Patch.

As long as the carnal mind remains in the heart of a regenerated man, he has to give the devil outlet.

For when the Christian loses his temper and smashes up things the devil is working his truck patch. It is like one man owning an acre of ground in the midst of a large plantation belonging to another man. The person that owns the acre can go through your plantation, sink a shaft, start a foundry and throw mud and slag all over your plantation. He may cause you a great deal of inconvenience, but as long as he owns a truck patch in your plantation he can go in and work his patch in spite of you, and no matter how fair your field, he is going to have outlet. Now, when you lose your temper and jerk off a singletree and knock your mule down, stamp the ground and pull your hair you are just giving him outlet and you see he is scattering mud and slag; and when you get mad in your home, jerk out a bench leg to hit your dog, grab the cat by the tail and throw it through the window, scold your wife, and slap one of your children, you are proving to the world that the devil has still got an outlet through your farm. Do you think you will ever grow him out?

I have seen a man in his field at work and becoming thirsty would call to his wife to bring him a drink. His wife in the house, the door closed and the children crying would fail to hear him. He would call the second time when she would come to the door and say:

"What is it, John?" He would yell like a wild Coman-che: "Where on earth is your ears? I have hollowed for an hour, until my throat is cracked open," when he had only called a time or two. If you were to ask them if they believed in Holiness they would say, "Oh, no, the Bible says there is none good, no not one, and I am a poor weak worm of the earth." You see the devil is still working his truck patch and getting out-let.

AN INFIDEL AND CRAMP COLIC.

I lived by an infidel once. He was the most foul mouthed man and had the sweetest little Christian wife I ever saw. He would make fun of religion most every day, when we met at the end of our rows at the field, but he was subject to the cramp colic. His wife would come over about once a month in great haste and say: "Bud, I believe Bill will die this time. He's got the worst spell of cramp colic he ever did have. You must come over and pray for him."

I'd go over and find him rolling from one side of the bed to the other, holding his stomach and saying: "Oh, Lord, if there be a Lord, have mercy on me, if there is any such thing as mercy."

I'd get on one side of the bed and Mary on the other, and pray for him and hold him on the bed. Along toward midnight he would get so bad he would leave out all the "ifs" and say: "Oh, Lord Jesus, you just must do something." He would finally get easy and go off to sleep. For the next few days when we would meet in the fields he would have nothing to say against religion. Toward the end of the week, when the soreness began to get out of his stomach, he would begin making fun of religion again. I would say: "All right, old boy, the Lord knows where you live, and he'll be around with another spell of cramp colic before long." He'd grin, clean off his plow and drive off, whistling through the field, saying: "Hit don't amount to nothin'." But inside of two years the cramp colic had brought him where we couldn't—to the altar—where I saw him stretched out in the straw one night, praying. You could have heard him a quarter of a mile away, and calling on his wife to have Brother Bud pray for him or he would be dead and in hell in a minute. I got down again on one side with Mary on the other. In a few minutes he was gloriously converted. He picked me up and hugged me and said: "Old boy, I always knew there was something in it," and went shouting all over the camp ground.

A STALL FED CALF.

Mal. 4:2: "But unto you that fear my name shall the sun of Righteousness arise," etc. The

Lord has a wonderful picture here when he likens the people to a stall-fed calf. But it is the man that fears his name. This text is addressed to the converted man—he who "fears God's name." The regenerated man serves God from a sense of duty. The sanctified man does it as a privilege. I am not going to heaven as a sense of duty, but as a privilege. "With healing in his wings." The man that fears God needs to be healed. The whole man—physical, mental and spiritual —fell with Adam. I don't care what you call me if the diseases of my soul are cured. The thing the Lord gave me I am going to keep. It is not on the market. Conversion does not cure the diseases of the soul. The Bible does not say so. When you hear a man say that he got it all when converted, he means he got all at that time that he did get. We believe in a perfect conversion, but conversion does not cure the disease of the soul. A man may be full of anger and not show it. There is a difference between a sullen possum and a dead possum. So there is a difference between repressed pride and pride that is destroyed. Conversion will not cure jealousy. A dead man does not need to be held down. Jealousy may be held down by conversion, but not destroyed. As a rule almost every unsanctified preacher is jealous of some one who can preach better than himself. Some folks call their spells nervousness. But I have had nervousness and I have had the other, and I know it is not nervousness. Some men try to excuse their spells by saying, "I always was of a positive make-up." But it is not that at all. In Texas there are three kinds of cattle: 1. Those who live on free grass. They are outsiders. They are lane runners. They are a hard-looking set. They represent the sinner. 2. Beautiful pasture fed cattle — marked and branded, plenty of grass and water. These represent the converted man. 3. The stall-fed calf. He looks better than the pasture fed cattle. He has plenty of feed—chopped feed. He is led out by the owner to show him off. This represents the sanctified people. I covet a strong body, but the thing we need most is a well soul.

The Day of His Wrath.

"Except ye repent, ye shall all likewise perish," and "Ye must be born again," and again, "Without holiness no man shall see the Lord," and "Nothing that defileth shall enter into the city." So you see the way in. Repentance leads to the new birth, and the new birth leads to holiness, and holiness leads into the city. Now my text is a very plain passage from Revelation 6:15-17. Many things in the Book tell of the rewards of the righteous and the wicked, according to their works. God looks at every step I take, and every desire I have,

and I must be clean or I can't go in.   There is a great
day ahead of all of us.   Some won't go in.   If he comes
here and knocks and I let him in, when I knock up
there he will let me in.   But if I don't let him in down
here, he won't let me in up there.   Isn't that fair?   I
don't want to go to hell, and I don't have to.   I want
to go to heaven.   I don't call myself a poor boy any
longer, for God calls me rich: "Ye, through his poverty,
become rich."   Well, a fellow that God calls rich can
afford to have a white tie, and a long-tailed coat, and
have his shoes shined once in a while.   Oh, the horror
of having God turn you away forever from the pure
and the good.   It would be like a literal hell of fire and
brimstone for me to have to dwell with the impure forever.   We can't afford to be on the left hand.   If you've
wronged a party, you don't want to meet him.   So those
that have wronged God cry for the rocks and the mountains to fall upon them.   "The great day of his wrath"
must be the "most awful of all days."   Now it is the
day of mercy.   There have been some awful days of
.wrath made manifest in different places, even on the
earth.   The story of the cross is a love story, an awful
tragedy.   God is long-suffering, not willing that any
should perish.   He has done everything for us he can.
I can't afford not to be prepared, not to have Christ.
I can't afford to come up with anything else than a clean

record. God sees you are worth a great deal, or he would not have paid such an enormous price for you. God is too much of a gentleman to come where he is not welcomed. What a fearful day that day of eternal separation! Oh, the price of having God is only a welcome. Do you extend a welcome to him.

THE MIND OF CHRIST.

I want to talk from a scripture that gives comfort to my soul, Phil. 2:1-16. This scripture shows Christ is to dwell in us. A man's fortune is made if he has got rid of carnality and put on Jesus. People want my experience, but they could not use it. The Lord got me down at the mourner's bench and took my measure, and gave me an experience which fitted me. My experience was made for a stuttering Irishman, and it would not fit you. You can not get the mind of Christ until you get rid of the carnal mind. You may be cross-eyed or have the rheumatism, but your trouble is below your collarbone and a little to the left of your stomach. You could cover it with a biscuit. It is the carnal mind. There is such a thing as not only getting converted, but having God reach down and pull out the carnal mind, and then you will have the mind of Jesus. Everybody in heaven will have the mind of Jesus. There are only two minds spoken of in the Bible— the spiritual and the carnal mind. A sinner has only one mind. He gets converted, then he gets the spiritual mind and is double-minded. Now your heart agrees with me if your head does not. Perhaps your head does not amount to much. The Lord does not say much about our head. You may dispute it, but what is there that has not been disputed! There is but one remedy for the carnal mind. It is described in Romans 6:6. My children came into the world with a trouble on hand —the carnal mind. Do you think you can be angry as a Christian and not have trouble? If you have no remedy for your angry spells you are in a bad fix. Anger is bad to go to the judgment with. Suppose you should have one of those spells at the judgment! Moving to another country does not change you. There is a warfare within. There could not be a warfare except there are two parties antagonistic. The carnal mind will act well in church and then have a spell at home. Why does he not act that way at church? Because he is your enemy. Have God take this carnal mind out of you and you will be happy. The holiness move is moving. It has three "gets" in it. It is get the blessing or get out of the way, or you will get run over. Some of us are going any way.

PERFECT LOVE.

I. Corinthians, second chapter, is the description of a sanctified man. The third chapter is a Christian not wholly sanctified. The text is, "Perfect love casts out fear." There are plenty of people preaching perfect love in heaven, but we get it here. If there is anything we need in this country, it is perfect love. It makes us bold. But some people mistake what boldness is. It does not mean to kill some one else who does not have it as we do. God has had such people all along through the ages. He says they had it, too. Noah had it. Abraham had it. God said, "Walk before me and be thou perfect." And Abraham was the friend of God and of course he had it. People derided Noah until the creek got up, and then they wanted to get into the boat. We can not be perfect in the sight of men. A man may be perfect in the sight of God and all wrong in the sight of men. A holy man in New York State had charges preferred against him. The bill of charges was longer than himself and the pastor said he was the best man he ever knew. Hezekiah claimed that he had "served God with a perfect heart." He asked God to remember it. And God said I will add fifteen years to his life. That is a pretty good addition to perfect love. He did not say, "I make many crooked paths and am a poor worm of the dust." I notice when you call on one of these tobacco worms to pray that they wind up with, "I am a poor worm of the dust." I saw a preacher coming down the street smoking a cigar, and it reminded me of what a young woman said to Jesus about her brother, "By this time he stinketh." Opium has been no greater curse to China than tobacco is to America. Somebody says, "You are a crank." Yes, but they always make cranks out of the best material. Job was a perfect man, and he had the blessing. The psalmist says, "Mark the perfect man and behold the upright, for the end of that man is peace." This peace runs from here to the New Jerusalem, and we do not want anything farther than that. Jesus said, "Be ye therefore perfect even as your Father which is in heaven is perfect." Some say that was not what he meant. Well, why did he not say what he meant, then?

SUCCESS OVER DIFFICULTIES.

One of the ways to succeed in life, when you meet with what the devil would call an impossibility, is to take the handspike of faith and turn the thing over and you will find a gold mine underneath. You can just fill your pockets and go on shining and shouting. When you meet with a difficulty just put the saddle of faith on him and ride him to the city of industry and tie him up to the post of success and pray down an old time revival that will cause men to run across Jordan, shout down Jericho, kill Achan and march up and take Ai. When you meet with a "surrounding circumstance" and the enemy says, "Now, just look at that," God will enable you to take the key of faith and walk up face to face with your circumstances, unlock the doors and go into his treasuries and you will find an old-fashioned Tennessee cupboard filled with the good things of life. Oh, yes, you will find grapes, pomegranates, old wheat and barley, milk and honey on every shelf, and you will have nothing to do but lick honey and drink milk, and shout while your enemies lick the dust and flee before you.

Well, glory to God, who said the devil was ahead? Not I. Well, bless your soul, don't you hear him say, "Fear not little flock, it is your Father's good pleasure to give you the kingdom." Bless the Lord, a kingdom surely puts man ahead of his circumstances. But some one may say, "What is a kingdom?" Let the Lord answer. Hear him. Romans 14:17: "For the kingdom of God is not meat and drink, but righteousness and peace and joy in the Holy Ghost." Well, hallelujah, a man with a kingdom has a fortune in two worlds; he is above sin and the devil in this and a stockholder in the New Jerusalem, and is a member of a great joint company that is known as the Upper Tens of the clouds, who make headquarters on the banks of the river of Life, dwelling under the tree of life, which yields her fruit every month in the year and its leaves are for the healing of the nations, who go with the noise of many waters, with the speed of lightning and in company with the angels and Jesus Christ at the head of the band. Praise the Lord, the fellow that is sucking seed is surely flying.

PROOF OF DEPRAVITY.

A few months ago in one of the little cities in Texas where I was preaching, a Methodist preacher sent for me to come to his study and talk with him. I went over at the appointed hour and met a very pleasant looking gentleman; looked to be about fifty years of age. In our conversation he told me he had gone through school, traveled abroad and read all the books, and had never seen, heard or felt anything that convinced him we Holiness people were right. He said the thing that we called the old man or the carnal mind did not exist. He said in proof of the fact: "Our children were born as pure as angels and as free from depravity as an archangel." I told him I could not believe my children were anything like angels. If my babies were a type of Heaven the war was not settled up there yet. "Well," he said; "Brother Robinson, you are honest in what you believe but your trouble is ignorance. You Holiness people know nothing of scholarship and you are under an awful delusion. You think this thing is so and I am sorry for you." I replied: "Brother, the people I've been raised with drink and swear, lie, steal, chew tobacco, fight and even kill. Now what on earth ails my kin folks?"

"Oh," he said, "they learned it from their parents." I replied, "Who did their parents learn it from?"

He said they were an uneducated people; that he admired me for my "git up and git" and heart of love and zeal, but you cry over the people just like they were in an awful condition. I replied: "They are."

"No," he said, "it is a delusion you Holiness people are under."

I said, "You surely believe these sinners of this country are on the road to an awful hell."

"No," he said, "that is your ignorance again. If the children of this country were brought up right they would not need anything at all." That he was brought up right and never needed a thing on earth that we Holiness people talked so much about.

I told him I was sorry I was brought up so poorly, but I was sure I needed everything God had for me. Our conversation closed late Saturday evening. On Monday evening following, at a church entertainment, he and a young man had a serious racket. In less than one month from this time this preacher got on a drunk, painted the town red, sent his credentials up to the

Presiding Elder and told him he had "found out religion was bosh."

"Now, reader, put on your spectacles and see if you
can find anything that would prove to you that the
human family was out of gear. I see things that convince me, but I don't know much. Now you look
over by a church racket and up the street and see a D.
D. on a whiz and see if you can see anything that makes
you think of angels.

THE MYSTERY OF GODLINESS.

Text, I. Tim., 3:16, "Great is the mystery of godli-
ness." In this one verse we have a complete history of
the Son of God. When men want to explain a thing
they generally take up two or three pages, and then
we do not know what they mean. When God wants us
to know a thing he tells us. People say, Brother Bud,
how do you explain that "God so loved the world that
he gave his only begotten Son?" Well, I don't try to
explain it. The text brings out the idea of God getting
down on a level with us. The only way God could help
us was to get down on a level with us. Jesus is light
and he comes down into me, and my soul is full of light.
Jesus found us starving and he came down to where
we lived to feed us. He knew that we were thirsty,
and he is the water of life. He found us without any

meat to go with the bread. He came to make us rich. "That we through his poverty might be rich." Since he came into my soul I have felt like one of the upper ten. When I hear people talk about the upper ten, I know who they mean. Don't you tell the people again that you are poor. In the country where we are going, gold is so cheap they have paved the streets with it. The man who is going there has not time to run a gold mine here. The thing that we have got is the best there is. The best the devil can get us here is whisky, cards, horse racing, etc. The devil tells his folks he is going to give them a good time. Well, when is it going to take place? Many are expecting to strike a streak. Well, they have a streak of damnation. We are representing God and he is our Father. He owns the cattle on a thousand hills, and all the potatoes in the hills. God manufactures satisfaction but he gives it to those who are his people. When you go out all day and come home tired, think of what Jesus says, "Come unto me all ye that labor and are heavy laden." Most people die in middle life because of worry. If you would just remember that you are only a piece of mud, and common mud, too, we would get along a good deal better. Get the principles of Jesus Christ in you and you will act as Jesus Christ would under the same circumstances. You can not trust God because of circumstances. The

Lord does not know anything about circumstances. You walk up the road arm in arm with God and you will never meet a circumstance. He makes us overcomers. Some one says, he makes us come overs. We come over all obstacles. Jesus began to make a mansion as soon as he went up to heaven and he is making us ready for the mansion at the same time. Some day the chariot will come and I will step aboard and go to it with the speed of lightning and not stop to say good-by to Venus or Jupiter as I go by. When Jesus was on earth he talked about the Father and when the Holy Ghost comes to us he will talk about Jesus, and when the Holy Ghost comes into us we will talk about them all. Jesus is coming. I do not know what train he is coming on, so we must have on our wedding dresses.

The Three Dispensations.

Under the dispensation of the Father, salvation was measured to us by the cup. The Psalmist said: "Thou anointest my head with oil, my cup runneth over." Under the dispensation of the Son we had wells of salvation. Our blessed Christ said in John 4:14: "The water that I shall give him shall be in him a well of water, springing up into everlasting life." Under the dispensation of the Holy Ghost we have salvation in rivers. Christ said in John 7: 38-39: "He that believeth on me as the scripture hath said out of his belly shall flow rivers of living water. But this spake he of the spirit which they that believe on him should receive, for the Holy Ghost was not yet given because that Jesus was not yet glorified."

Everything seems to come to us in trinities or trios, both good and evil. We have on our side the Father, Son and Holy Ghost. We have against us the world, the flesh and the devil. We have God the Father to overcome the world with, Jesus Christ to overcome the devil with and the blessed Holy Ghost to burn out the flesh with. Well, glory to God, they that be for us are more than they that be against us.

We next notice that the grace of God comes to us in trios. Paul says: "And now abideth faith, hope and love, these three, but the greatest of these is love."

Now the works of the devil are manifold in a three-fold manner. In 1st John 2:16 we have, "For all that there is in the world, the lust of the flesh, and the lust of the eyes, and the pride of life is not of the Father, but is of the world." Now, you see, friend, we have all the combined forces of earth and hell to fight and let's see to it at once that we "put on the whole armor of God, that we may be able to stand against the wiles of the devil, for we wrestle not against flesh and blood, but against powers, against the rulers of this world, against spiritual wickedness in high places, wherefore take unto you the whole armor of God, that ye may be able to withstand in the evil day, and having done all to stand.   Stand therefore having your loins **girt** about with the truth and having on the breastplate of righteousness and your feet shod with the preparation of the gospel of peace."

We next notice that there are three places of abode spoken of in the Bible: this world, heaven and hell. At present we are in this world, in a short time we will be either in heaven or hell. A life of righteousness and holiness will prepare you for a home in heaven with God and the angels and the redeemed saints of all ages, while a life of sin and unbelief will prepare you to spend a life with the devil and the lost in an awful hell.

Then we have three classes of people: the first is the condemned sinner; the second is the justified child of God; the third is the wholly sanctified Christian. The sinner does not fear God or serve him at all; while the justified person serves God from a sense of duty and fear; and the sanctified from a sense of love and privilege.

THE BLOOD OF CHRIST.

Read Hebrews, ninth chapter. Everything in the Bible runs to the blood as the basis of salvation.

Notice a moment Christ as God's Lamb "without blemish," "slain from the foundation of the world." Jesus carried his cross, as Isaac carried the wood on his shoulder. Isaac was Abraham's well-beloved son. So Israel is called God's first-born, and they were required, you remember, to sprinkle blood on the door-posts, and the angel passed over them. Peter says, 1 Pet. i, 18-20, no head-work, nor hand-work, nor feet-work will do, no "corruptible things," but only the precious blood. Oh, it's so good, it's nearly tickling me to death to tell you about it. Oh, to be "under the blood." The only way God can forgive sins is through his blood, "according to the riches of his grace." God keeps me in the hollow of his hand, and once in a while, when I have trials and troubles, God lifts his hand and looks in and says "He's a-keeping all right." Well, if you are under the blood, you'll be level-headed. Salvation won't give you a college education, but it will enable you to use what sense you have got. It may not keep a man from snoring, but it will help him to get up on the right side of the bed. It is only the merits of the crucified Savior that will avail. We need to be sanctified to be kept justified. A justified and sanctified yardstick are both 36 inches long. You can't keep justified long without getting sanctified, or else you'll go back. You need the golden pot of a sanctified heart to keep the snow-white honey sweet manna of a justified experience in. The outward life of justification and sanctification are the same. The folks going to heaven are to have an easy time going there, according to God's order. The folks going to hell have the hard time. Cleansing of the church is what Christ died for. You need not a little more justification, or to die a little deader. A dead man don't kick if you stick a pin in his heel. Holiness, sanctification, perfection, election and victory are all through the blood, as you see from different scripture verses. The Holy Ghost was never given until the blood was shed. When I was a candidate for the New Jerusalem the devil wasn't allowed to vote, but the Father, Son and Holy Ghost voted for me, and the angels counted the ballots and found it unanimous, and they went to shouting up there, and I went to shouting down here. I have been elected. I know when I was a candidate and when I ran and when I was voted for. It came through the blood. The holiness people are the elect. It is the only election that the devil has nothing to do with. It takes an elect man to overcome the devil.

Nothing we need more than the blood of Jesus Christ. It will wash the soul from sin, and such a man will have a clean heart. I am so glad we have the blood to-day. When I came in contact with Jesus he washed me sky-blue, and snow-white, and blood-red. I was out in the woods praying, and I asked the Lord what it meant to be kept in the hollow of his hand. So I closed my hand and then opened it a little and looked in. And that is what God did for me. He put his hand over me and looked in and said, "He'll keep."

The blood is the price of his redemption. "Even the forgiveness of our sins." I do not know what the word "even" means (I am not a scholar) unless it means that it brings up a feller like me and brings another down on a level with me. It makes us even. We are justified through the blood. Every man thus justified is a member of the church, which he bought with his blood. If the church is alive and I throw rocks at it, I may knock out an eye or break a leg. If it is dead and I throw stones at it, I am stoning a corpse. I show I have no sense. Most of the religious people are hungry for a better experience. All live children are hungry. As long as I walk in the light he makes me clean. I do the washing and he does the cleansing. The devil can't tell worse things about me than I can about him. And unless he keeps still I'll tell on him. Conversion leads you into the holy place, and the blood enables you to enter into the holiest place. If you have got true religion you will act just as God would if he were in your place.

The Two Works of Grace.

It is remarkable how plain some things are made in the Bible, and yet some people that claim a large quantity of brains and a good deal of grace deny the two works of grace that are taught in the Bible. I have heard them say so often: "Oh, I believe in sanctification as strong as you do, but the two works of grace is what we deny. We believe that we get it all in conversion, and we don't believe the Lord ever does a half job on a fellow; we believe we get everything in conversion that the second blessing fanatics claim to have."

Well, now my dear friends, if I can't prove to you out of your own Bible that you did not get sanctification in conversion I will obligate myself to sit down in your presence and just eat your Bible up from Genesis to Revelation and lick up the backs without sugar or salt on it. Now, just listen to what your Bible says. Take the two prayers of our blessed Savior and compare them and if you will be honest with God and with your own soul and your Bible you will have to say that converting sinners and sanctifying believers are two different works of grace. Take the first prayer of our blessed Lord and see just what he says. Luke 23:34. Now hear him: "Then said Jesus, Father, forgive them for they know not what they do." Now readers, if conversion and sanctification is the same, why did not the Christ of

Calvary say, Father, sanctify them, for they know not what they do? Oh, no readers, you can't think of the mob that nailed our Lord to the tree and gambled over his coat at the foot of the cross, seeking the blessing of sanctification, and you know it. Now hear the second prayer. Read John 17:9: "I pray for them. I pray not for the world" (or for sinners, as the world in this place means unsaved people). "They are not of the world," John 17:16. This verse proves that they were not sinners, and if you believe a word in your Bible from beginning to end you will have to confess that if they were not sinners they were Christians. Christ said in the ninth verse that he wasn't praying for the world. Well, if they were not sinners what did Christ want them to have. Just read the seventeenth verse and see: "Sanctify them through thy truth; thy word is truth." Now, neighbor, you have the two prayers offered by the Savior for two classes of people. In the first prayer he said, "Father, forgive them." In the second prayer he says, "Father sanctify them." Now just look at the difference between the two prayers and between the two crowds prayed for. The first prayer was offered for the rough rabble that were driving nails into his hands and feet, casting lots upon his garment, wagging their heads and mocking him while he died. The second prayer was offered for his disciples up in

the upper room just after they had eaten the passover
and he had instituted the Lord's supper, washed their
feet and had his last conversation with them recorded
in the fourteenth, fifteenth, sixteenth and seventeenth
chapters of John's gospel. These are the same men that
he had just said had their names written in Heaven—
Luke 10:20—and any fair-minded man or woman, black
or white, anywhere in the United States, knows that
this conversation referred to in John's gospel was not
between Christ and a mob of sinners. Now, friend, if
you can't see that one of these prayers was for one object
and the other for another, just get out your old Bible
and I will lick her up.

A TYPE OF CHRIST AND THE CHURCH.

I have seen the husband leave his home in one of our
little towns and go off to the city to work and sometimes
stay several months preparing a home, and finally he
wires his wife he will be there on the next train. His
wife gets the message and her heart all aglow to think
of the return of her husband; she gets the children
ready, and at least an hour before train time she has
every child washed and dressed in their best clothes
and is off to meet the train. She takes the baby in her
arms, leads the next least one and puts two or three
little fellows before her and starts in a trot for the

depot. Every few steps she is hurrying them up, saying: "Come on sugar pie, papa is coming home," and her little heart is not concerned about anything but reaching the depot. As she goes down the street the dressmaker calls out to her: "Silk dresses are two dollars cheaper than they were last week," but she pays no attention to silk dresses, she is going to meet her husband. A little farther down the street another woman calls out, "Hats, fifty cents off to-day. Ostrich feathers seventy-five cents a piece," but she don't hear anything that is going on in the business world. She is dead to everything but meeting the bridegroom. She reaches the station and says to the porter: "When is the train due?" He answers, "In ten minutes." She walks the floor, looks out at the windows and listens for the train. The ten minutes seem like hours. As the train whistles she is on the platform with every one of the babies, telling the little fellows to wave their handkerchiefs at the train, that papa is coming home. As the train pulls in her face shines, her eyes sparkle, and she says to the children, Do you see him? He is looking out of the window. The porter says, "Stand back and give the passengers a chance to get off," but she pays no attention to the porter, she is going to meet her husband. As he steps to the platform she is in his arms with all of the babies, and one smile from him and a few kind

words is worth more to her than all the silk and feathers
in the world. She has met the ideal of her life and is
satisfied.

Now, friend, how different this picture would have
been if while her husband was away she had proven untrue and had gone to flirting with the world. Do you
suppose she would have rejoiced when she received the
telegram? Or do you think she would have gone to the
depot with the children? Not much. She would have
sulked around and said, "It disturbs my peace to hear
of his coming back." Yes, she would rather hear of
anything in the world than to hear of the return of the
bridegroom. Why? Because she has proven untrue.

So with the church. When the sanctified bride of
Christ hears of his return her face shines and she begins
to dress up the children and sing and shout and look
for the train. But take the unsanctified part of the
church and say anything to them about the second coming of Christ and you have trouble on your hands. The
look of dissatisfaction and unrest mingled with con-
tempt and disgust proves clearly to your mind the bride
has lost her first love and has gone to flirting with the
world. If you belong to the church and the church belongs to Christ and he has gone to prepare a home for
his bride, on what grounds could you reject his return
and retain your salvation, for He said: "If I go and

prepare a place for you I will come again and receive you unto myself. Where I am there ye may be also and whither I go ye know and the way ye know."

Christ Is All In All.

There are some things Christ says about himself and some things he is to us that are very précious to my heart.

"In the beginning was the Word, and the Word was with God and the Word was God. The same was in the beginning with God.

"All things were made by Him, and without Him was not anything made that was made. In Him was life, and the life was the light of men.

"And the light shineth in darkness and the darkness comprehended it not.

"He was in the world and the world was made by him, and the world knew him not. He came unto his own and his own received him not.

"But as many as received him to them gave he power to become the sons of God, even to them that believe on his name.

"Which were born not of blood nor of the will of the flesh, nor of the will of man, but of God. And the Word was made flesh and dwelt among us."

We see he is the Word and he says, "I am come that

they might have life." He says, "I am the life; I am the light of the world."

Then he says, "I am the bread of life. This is the bread which cometh down from Heaven that a man may eat thereof and not die."

"I am the water of life." "In the last day, that great day of the feast, Jesus stood and cried saying: If any man thirst let him come unto me and drink. The water that I shall give him shall be in him a well of water springing up into everlasting life."

He says he will give rest. When we have life, food and water we naturally need rest. He says:

"Come unto me all ye that labor and are heavy laden and I will give you rest. Take my yoke upon you and learn of me, for I am meek and lowly in heart and ye shall find rest unto your souls, for my yoke is easy and my burden is light."

Here we find the two rests—rest from the burden of sin and guilt and the rest from self by taking his yoke and becoming meek and lowly. Then comes sleep. And so he gives his beloved sleep. After a day's work there is nothing so refreshing and sweet as a few hours sleep, and when we wake in the morning we want the way. He says: "I am the way." We find the way through the tomb, and he says: "I am the truth." He says: "I am the good shepherd. The good shepherd giveth his life for the sheep." How can the sheep go in and out and find pasture without a door? Behold he says: "I am the door; by me if any man enter in he shall be saved and shall go in and out and find pasture."

Now, back behind all of these is our redemption. "In whom we have redemption through his blood, the forgiveness of sins, according to his riches of grace." Now, after having our sins forgiven we need to have the sin of our nature taken away, and we hear John say: "Behold the lamb of God, which taketh away the sin of the world."

We are now ready to go in and possess the land and come into the inheritance of our riches. We find our riches in him. "For ye know the grace of our Lord Jesus Christ, that though he was rich, yet for your sakes he became poor that ye through his poverty might be rich. But my God shall supply all your need according to his riches in glory by Christ Jesus."

And being in possession of these great riches, we need wisdom to guide our affairs discreetly. We will come to Jesus again, in whom are hid all the treasures of wisdom and knowledge.

"And ye are complete in him which is the head of all principalities and powers. For in him dwelleth all the fullness of the Godhead bodily."

"But of him are ye in Christ Jesus, who of God, is

made unto us wisdom and righteousness and sanctification and redemption."

Well, glory to God, the next platform we light on is that of peace, and like all other blessings, we get it from our blessed Christ. About the last thing he willed us before leaving was his peace. "Peace I leave with you. My peace I give unto you. Not as the world giveth give I unto you. Let not your heart be troubled, neither let it be afraid." "And the work of righteousness shall be peace and the effect of righteousness quietness and assurance forever."

"And my people shall dwell in a peaceable habitation and in sure dwellings and in quiet resting places," for "Great peace have they which love thy law and nothing shall offend them," for "Thou wilt keep him in perfect peace whose mind is stayed on thee because he trusteth in thee."

Then we have, "Be careful for nothing, but in everything by prayer and supplication with thanksgiving let your requests be made known unto God. And the peace of God which passeth all understanding shall keep your hearts and minds through Christ Jesus."

ABOUNDING GRACE.

Paul says in Romans 5:20, "Moreover the law entered, that the offense might abound. But where sin abounded, grace did much more abound." The contrast, you see, is between grace and sin, and Paul declares that God has a greater quantity of grace than the devil has of sin. God has abundance of grace and the devil has a meager supply of sin. He is scattering it profusely over the country at present, but the day is not far in the future when he will not be allowed to put a foot in our beautiful land. My blessed Christ will bring the angels and they will chain him and lead him away and shut him up in his dark pit. But thank God, grace will roll on like a mighty ocean forever. Well, glory to God, it makes me just shout to think of it! It is the finest thing in this world. This is not a vain delusion of mine, but God says it is so, and I will believe it or die. Hallelujah! The real meaning of the text is just this: The supply is greater than the demand, or the plaster is larger than the sore. If you have a piece of sin on you as big as my hand, God has a piece of grace as big as a bed quilt to spread over it. Well, glory! Or to make it real plain: If the country in which you live has a blotch on it as big as a mud hole in the road, God has a piece of grace as big as a 640-acre farm to cover it up with. Sin is limited, grace is not. Sin is the offspring of the devil. Grace is the offspring of God. Sin can't rise any higher than its fountain head —and we know that is hell. Grace can rise as high as

its fountain head, and that is in Heaven, and, thank
God, Heaven is above hell. God is greater in his resources than the devil is in his. In proof of the fact.
Sin will make a man curse. Grace will make him shout.
Sin makes him hate his neighbor. Grace makes him
love his neighbor as himself. Sin is degrading to manhood. Grace is elevating. Sin will take a nice sweet
boy out of your home, put him down in slumdom and
put him to feeding the devil's hogs and really put him
below the brute family. Grace will go down there, get
that boy and bring him out, wash him up, put clean
clothes on him and make one of the most respectable
young gentlemen in the country out of him. This proves
that the resources of grace are inexhaustible.

I will make it plainer than that. Now just hold your
head open a minute and listen while I talk. I remember doing a day's work for the devil. I worked hard
all day. I ate yellow corn bread and pumpkin and
drank water out of a mud hole and slept on straw,
dreamed of dying and going to hell, fought with devils
all night and waked next morning tired and weary. I
thought my liver was out of fix and I needed a dose
of Carter's little liver pills. What a delusion!

I remember doing another day's work. I did not
work as hard as I did the first day. I preached three
times, rode to church in a fine carriage, I had sirloin

steak, graham toast, and celery, Jersey butter, Irish potatoes mashed up with butter, a bowl of strawberries by my plate and plenty of rich Jersey milk. At night I rolled about on goose feathers under blankets made of real sheep wool, dreamed of beautiful mountains, rivers, rainbows, lovely cities and angels, awoke next morning with my heart and liver both clean and nice. I felt perfectly rested and knew that while I slept the angels had been fanning me with the breezes of heaven. I wanted to put one arm around Jesus Christ and the other around the whole world and bring them together. As I was fixing to start the next morning the preacher in charge of the church where I had preached, put three five-dollar bills into my hand and said, "May God be with you, my brother; you have been a great blessing to me and my people. I am sorry we have so little on hand for you this morning."

Now, reader, if you can't see a difference between these two days' work, you couldn't see through a hogshead with both heads knocked out.

Some Bible Characters.

Adam sinned and lost Eden.

Cain was the first murderer.

Enoch walked with God and was translated, and was the father of the oldest man that ever lived.

Methuselah lived to be nine hundred and sixty-nine years old.

Noah built the ark and escaped the deluge.

Abraham offered up Isaac and was the friend of God and father of the faithful.

Lot separated from Abraham, pitched his tent toward Sodom, fled from the burning city with the loss of everything but two children.

Isaac was the father of the first twins recorded.

Jacob was the father of the twelve patriarchs.

Joseph was the type of Christ; the beautiful dreamer. He wore a coat of many colors. He was sold by his brethren for twenty pieces of silver, the price of a slave under age. He served fourteen years in Potipher's prison, came out to rule Egypt, the greatest nation then in the world.

Moses led Israel out of Egyptian bondage; was the meekest man that ever lived. He died on Mt. Nebo and was buried by the Lord. We have no news of his coming back for fourteen hundred and fifty years, when he came down and spent the night with the Lord on the Mount of Transfiguration.

Joshua and Caleb spied out the land of Canaan.

Caleb said, "We are well able to overcome it; let us go up and possess it." But the other ten preachers said we be grasshoppers in our sight and in their sight.

Joshua led Israel through Jordan into Canaan, blew down Jericho with the ram's horn, killed Achan, took Ai and ruled Israel twenty-four years; died, being a hundred and ten years old.

Shamgar killed six hundred Philistines with an ox goad.

Deborah was the first woman that ever ruled Israel.

Balaam was the only man that ever owned a talking donkey.

Gideon took three hundred men with twenty pitchers and lamps in them and broke the pitchers and put to flight the Midianites that were like grasshoppers for multitude.

Samson caught three hundred foxes, set their tails on fire and turned them loose in the Philistines' corn fields and burned them up; he slew a thousand Philistines with the jaw bone of an ass; he broke the cords and withes, pulled up the gate posts, and ran away with the loom swinging to the locks of his head, but he backslid and his enemies bound him and put out his eyes and made him make sport for them. When a preacher backslides the devil sends him out to make sport for the people. Samson with his eyes open was a terror to his enemies, with them out he made sport for them. So with the preachers of all ages.

Samuel's mother lent him to the Lord when he was

weaned, and he never departed from the house of the Lord. From the time he was six years old the Lord revealed his secrets to him.

Saul, the son of Kish, was the first King of Israel. He was head and shoulders above his brethren. He was a great warrior and chosen of God, but forsook the Lord, sought witches and committed suicide.

King David succeeded Saul as King of Israel and was a man after God's own heart. He slew Goliath, the Philistine giant, with a pebble from his sling. He was the greatest general the world ever saw and the sweet singer of Israel.

Solomon, the son of David, was the wisest man that ever lived; ruled Israel in the time of his father, and was chosen of God to build the Temple, the only house we have any record of that was ever built without the sound of a hammer.

Isaiah was the gospel preacher of the old dispensation, and wrote the obituary of Jesus Christ seven hundred and twelve years before he was born. History says he was a martyr for his faith in God and was sawed asunder.

Jeremiah was the weeping prophet, and saw the church in a state of apostasy, and compared it to a piece of clay in the hand of the potter that was marred on the wheel. The elders became enraged and cast him into the dungeon, and he sank down in the mire and was lifted out by an Ethiopian.

Ezekiel was one of the greatest prophets of the old dispensation. The modern preachers tell us they get all the inspiration they need from the faces of their congregation on Sunday morning, but suppose Ezekiel would have depended upon the inspiration he got from his congregation. His sermon surely would have been dry, for he had nothing to begin with but a valley of dry bones, and even the Lord said, "Son of man, can these bones live?" And he said, "Lord God, thou knowest." He was blessed with the privilege of seeing the river of Life flowing out from beneath the throne of God.

For a living faith in a mighty God, Daniel and the three Hebrew children have never been surpassed. Shadrach, Meshach and Abednego walked through the burning fiery furnace and came out without the smell of fire. The reason they did not burn; they had been burned out. Daniel read the "handwriting on the wall," revealed to the King his wonderful vision, stayed all night in the lion's den and came out without a scratch, all because he had purposed in his heart not to defile himself with meat from the King's table.

Hosea was one of the minor prophets and a sweet

writer in Israel. He wrote a beautiful letter to a back-slidden church, but she didn't repent.

Joel wrote only a short sketch—three chapters—but he had the privilege of looking down the stream of time eight hundred years and seeing the mighty pentecost flooding the world with the Holy Ghost.

Amos writes the necessity of God's judgments against Israel and the certainty of Israel's desolation, and pictures the famine that was to be in the land, not for bread or water, but for the hearing of the words of the Lord.

Jonah has a mighty following today. The Lord told him to go to Nineveh, but he started to Tarshish. As disobedience brings trouble, so he didn't run far until he was swallowed by a whale. He traveled three days and nights in the mighty deep without a ship. He finally made the landing and started for Nineveh. The last we heard of him he was under a gourd vine pouting because he got the whole city to the mourners' bench and God wouldn't destroy them, although God delivered him when he found an altar of prayer in the bosom of the deep.

> Whales there are on every side,
> With their mouths all open wide;
> Watch, my friend, to God be true,
> Or a whale will swallow you.

Obadiah writes only one chapter, but he preaches a mighty sermon on the pride and deceitfulness of the human heart.

The vision of Micah is beautiful. He looked through the telescope of time for more than seven hundred years and saw the glory of the church, the birth of Christ, his victory over his enemies and the church's final triumph.

Nahum was blessed with a twofold vision of Christ. He saw him in his first and second coming. In his first vision he says, "Behold, upon the mountains the feet of him that bringeth good tidings; that publisheth peace." In his second vision he looked down through the ages and saw the Salvation Army with their red jackets on, girdling the earth, and the electric cars flying through the streets, and calls this "the day of his preparation," i. e., "The shield of his mighty men is made red, the valiant men are scarlet. The chariots shall be with flaming torches in the day of his preparation and the fir tree shall be terribly shaken. The chariots shall rage in the streets, they shall jostle one against another in the broadways; they shall seem like torches; they shall run like the lightnings." Chap. 2:3, 4.

Habakkuk was not only a great Holiness preacher, but one of the greatest temperance lecturers of his day, and a believer in the Millennial reign of Christ. He had the kind of Holiness that goes clear through with the

Lord, and didn't depend upon circumstances for his experience. "Although the fig tree shall not blossom, neither shall there be fruit in the vines. The labor of the olive shall fail and the fields shall yield no meat. The flocks shall be cut off from the fold and there shall be no herd in the stalls."

"Yet I will rejoice in the Lord. I will joy in the God of my salvation."

"The Lord God is my strength and he will make me to walk upon mine high places." 3:17, 18, 19.

If the fig tree doesn't blossom he will have no figs. If the vines don't bear he will have no grapes. If the olive fails there will be no oil, and the fields yielding no meat, will leave him, literally, without bread. If the flocks are cut off there is no milk and butter, and when there are no herds in the stall there is no meat, yet he means to rejoice in the God of his salvation. You see he is delivered from this world.

As a temperance lecturer he is hard on the saloon-keeper or those who serve wine on their tables, for he says, "Woe unto him that buildeth a town with blood, and establisheth a city by iniquity. Woe unto him that giveth his neighbor drink, that puttest the bottle to him and makest him drunken also. Thou art filled with shame for glory, and shameful spewing shall be on thy glory."

"Because thou hast spoiled many nations all the rem- nants of the people shall spoil thee, because of men's blood and for the violence of the land." He believed Jesus would come conquering and to conquer. "For the earth shall be filled with the knowledge of the glory of the Lord as the waters cover the sea." To his broad statement concerning the Millennium, see second chap- ter Habakkuk.

Zephaniah calls Jerusalem to repentance, exhorts them to wail for the salvation of Israel. In his last chapter he breaks forth in rejoicing and puts the daugh- ters of Zion to singing and shouting, saying: "For the Lord thy God is in the midst of thee." 3:17.

Haggai declares that because the people live in good houses and failed to build the Lord a house that they should eat and not have enough, drink and not be filled, be clothed and not be warmed. They should earn wages and put them in bags with holes in them, because of his house that was waste and they ran every man to his own house. He would shut up the Heaven from dew and the earth from bringing forth fruit and would call for a drought upon the land. Upon the mountains, land and oil, upon men and cattle and all the labors of their hands. This should be a warning to all God's people to look after his house first.

Zechariah was the greatest of the minor prophets. In

his visions he saw the redemption of Zion, and Christ as the "Branch." The golden candlesticks, with his seven lamps; the two olive trees standing by it. The flying roll, the four chariots; the two mountains of brass and the Kingdom of the Branch, or the reign of Christ.

"And the Lord shall be King over all the earth. In that day shall there be one Lord and his name one." He says in chapter 14:20-21, and "In that day shall there be upon the bells of the horses Holiness unto the Lord, and the pots in the Lord's house shall be like the bowls before the altar. Yea every pot in Jerusalem and in Judah shall be Holiness unto the Lord."

He saw worse cranks about Holiness than we are.

Malachi was the last prophet of the Old Bible. He finished his prophesies three hundred and ninety-seven years before Christ, and left us to grope our way in darkness for nearly four hundred years. In the first and second chapters he gives us the picture of a back-slidden church and priests offering polluted bread and the blind, lame and sick as sacrifices. In the third chapter he shows us the whole nation robbing God of tithes and offerings, and promises if they will bring them in he will bless them until they can't contain the blessing, opening the windows of Heaven and pouring it out upon them. He also describes in this chapter the forerunner of Christ, the day of Pentecost and the sanctifying of the preachers. In verse three he beautifully describes the latter. "And he shall sit as a refiner and purifier of silver and he shall purify the sons of Levi and purge them as gold and silver, that they may offer unto the Lord an offering in righteousness." Malachi was surely a Holiness fellow from the way he believed in testimony. He declares that, "They that feared the Lord spake often one to another and the Lord hearkened and heard it and a book of remembrance was written before him for them that feared the Lord and that thought upon his name." 3:16. In the fourth chapter and second verse he describes the people of God as calves of the stall. "But unto you that fear my name shall the Sun of righteousness arise with healing in his wings, and ye shall go forth and grow up as calves of the stall." Thank God for the blessed privilege of being stall-fed calves.

God's Ability to Supply Our Needs.

"And God is able to make all grace abound toward you; that ye, always having all sufficiency in all things, may abound to every good work." 2nd Cor., 9:8.

There are enough "alls" in this scripture for every shoemaker in the world to have one. God stands behind every one of them, and they are all pointed toward you.

A great many people do not think He is able to supply all their needs, but I believe he is, and I want to talk about the abundant supplies he has on hand. He is "able to make all grace abound toward you; that ye, always having all sufficiency in all things, may abound to every good work."

Now let us see if He is able to do for us exactly what is needed. The first thing we need, as a lost world, is God's mercy. Has he a plentiful or a meager supply? The Book tells us that He has great quantities. Peter writes to the "elect according to the foreknowledge of God the Father, through the sanctification of the Spirit, unto obedience and sprinkling of the blood of Jesus Christ, grace unto you and peace be multiplied. Blessed be the God and Father of our Lord Jesus Christ; which, according to His abundant mercy, hath begotten us again unto a lively hope by the resurrection of Jesus Christ from the dead, to an inheritance incorruptible and undefiled, and that fadeth not away, reserved in Heaven for you, who are kept by the power of God through faith unto salvation ready to be revealed in the last time." 1st Peter, 1:2-5.

Notice in the third verse where He speaks of His abundant mercy. That abundance is something like the Atlantic Ocean, or the Rocky Mountains, or the prairies in Texas. You ask, "How big are those prairies?" Well, there's hardly any end to it. I can get in at my door and ride hundreds and hundreds of miles and see nothing but prairie land. And that is the way God talks about his mercy.

Is there anything else we need? What would we do if we had nothing else but mercy? Think what pardon means to a world condemned. Without it what would have become of me? So God likes mercy and pardon, and they make a fine composition.

Isaiah says: "Seek ye the Lord while he may be found; call ye upon him while He is near. Let the wicked forsake his ways and the unrighteous man his thoughts; and let him return unto the Lord and He will have mercy upon him; and to our God for He will abundantly pardon." Isaiah 55:6-7. And he goes on to say in that chapter: "For my thoughts are not your thoughts, neither are your ways my ways, saith the Lord. For as the Heavens are higher than the earth, so are my ways higher than your ways, and my thoughts than your thoughts. For as the rain cometh down and the snow from Heaven and returneth not hither, but watereth the earth, and maketh it bring forth and bud, that it may give seed to the sower and bread to the eater. So shall my word be that goeth forth out of my mouth; it shall not return unto me void, but it shall accomplish that which I please, and shall prosper in the things whereto I sent it. For ye shall go out with joy, and be led forth with peace; the mountains and the hills shall break forth before you into singing, and all the trees of the field shall clap their hands. Instead of the thorn shall come up the fir tree and instead of the brier shall come up the myrtle tree, and it shall be to the Lord for a name, for an everlasting sign that shall not be cut off."

Drop back to the tenth verse. "As the rain cometh down and the snow from Heaven, and returneth not thither, but watereth the earth and maketh it bring forth and bud, that it may give seed to the sower, and bread to the eater." Here let us stop a moment and think of the greatness of God. He has undertaken to feed this world. The whole human family, with all the birds and beasts, fish and insects, would all be dead in twelve months if the Lord did not produce enough food for them. For everything in the world is within twelve months of starvation.

If the Lord did not create anything else everything in the world would be eaten up in twelve months. Look at the fowls; where do they get their food? And the people of the earth. It must take at least nine hundred thousand loaves of bread a day to feed this town of six hundred thousand inhabitants, and about six hundred thousand pounds of meat. Where are you going to get this great quantity of food? The people of the land are complaining of the drought and the shortness of the crops, yet our markets are groaning under the burdens of meat and bread. And where do we get the material to make clothing for this world? Why, the Lord God has created it. There isn't a man in the world with brains or skill enough to make one Irish potato, or the material to make one pair of breeches. Now you infidels, agnostics and skeptics go and butt your brains out against the wall and get out of the way. If seed potatoes were lost tonight there isn't an infidel that walks the earth that could make an Irish potato and put the germ of life into it. God has to make it, and He can do it. He said: "Let there be light, and there was light." And He said: "Let there be potatoes," and they came rolling out from under the hills. We have a very poor conception of the ability of God. We think such men as McKinley and Bryan great men. Why, God is running the world; yes, and ten thousand other worlds bigger and greater than this.

Now, He has an abundant mercy and pardon for a lost world, and he says he is able to make all grace abound toward you. Isn't He doing this? If you don't love him tonight, I beseech you as an honest man to lay down your foolishness, or quit eating his bread, sleeping on his beds, wearing his clothes, and talking about him, as you think, behind his back. He is looking at you. In Genesis 16:13 we read, "Thou God seest me," and in Hebrews 4:12 it says, "The word of God is quick and powerful and sharper than any two-edged sword, piercing even to the dividing asunder of soul and spirit, and of the joints and marrow, and is a discerner of the thoughts and intents of the heart." Then if you will keep these two thoughts before you, you will quit sinning tonight. Every sin you commit you will have to meet it somewhere, and settle for it. Render unto Cæsar the things that are Cæsar's and unto God the things that are God's. So said our blessed Master. He knows how you live and he will show you every act of your life, and you will have to settle for it somewhere. If not here, at the judgment, and then it will be too late to make restitution.

At the great convention in Chicago, where there were a thousand conversions and sanctifications, men paid from a nickel to twelve hundred dollars in making restitution. Boys paid a nickel to the street car company for a stolen ride, and people paid up old debts, and more than twenty-five hundreds dollars were paid back of stolen money.

Last summer at Sunset, Texas, a converted—yes, a sanctified—man had something to straighten up. About fifteen years ago he stole a water barrel, and had for-

gotten all about. it. But he went out into the woods
and got down to pray when he heard a racket, and looking up, saw a water barrel rolling down the hill at him.
He said, "Lord, what's the matter with me?" And he
supposed it was an imagination, and went further down
the hollow and began to pray again, when he heard a
racket like a span of horses running away, and he looked
up and to his surprise it was the water barrel rolling
down again. And then he remembered that he had
stolen a water barrel from his neighbor about fifteen
years before that. He came back to the camp ground
and confessed it and sent the man one dollar for the
barrel and ten per cent interest. And he shouted all
over the camp ground. That wasn't much, you say.
No, but it took that to ease his conscience. You've got
to settle here in this country. It's much easier to settle
here than there.

But I started out to show all that God could do for
us. We read in Romans 5 :17, "For if by one man's
offense death reigned by one, much more they which
receive abundance of grace and the gift of righteousness shall reign in life by one Jesus Christ." This
shows that God has an abundance of grace. And in
the 20th verse, we read: "Where sin abounded, grace
did much more abound." This shows you law and
grace. The law is like an electric light to light up the

city. A man is wandering in the darkness, and he don't know where he is at nor the direction he is traveling, but suddenly the great electric light flashes out over his head and it locates him. It shows him exactly what part of the city he is in, and the direction he is traveling, and the filth and mud on the streets; but it has no power to stop him and turn him around and start him in the right direction. The electric light here takes the place of the law. The law will locate and show you just where you are, and through the law he can reveal to us the exceeding sinfulness of sin, and the exceeding richness of grace. That is a beautiful thought: "That where sin abounded, grace did much more abound." There is more grace than sin. The plaster is bigger than the sore. The supply is greater than the demand. So now we see he has an abundance of mercy, of pardon and grace.

That brings us to another thought. Go to Titus 3:5-6' and we read: "Not by works of righteousness which we have done, but according to his mercy he saved us, by the washing of regeneration, and renewing of the Holy Ghost, which he shed on us abundantly through Jesus Christ our Lord." He said he would shed the Holy Ghost on us abundantly, and would cover us with the shadow of his wings, and give us a river to swim in. We read in the forty-seventh chapter of Ezekiel

that he saw a river coming out from under the throne
of God, and he undertook to measure it and he measured
a thousand cubits, and it was up to his ankles; and he
measured a thousand cubits further and it was up to his
knees; and he measured a thousand cubits further and
it was up to his loins; and he measured a thousand
cubits further and it was a river that no man could
cross, and he had water to swim in. God has an abundance of just such things as you and I need, and some
of you go around with a hungry heart and a sad face
when you ought to have a shine on your face. My
friend, why don't you throw away your spoon and
jump into the river and let the Lord satisfy the crav-
ings of your hungry soul? When I was seeking the
blessing of sanctification, I would pray for the Lord
to come in all his might and power and to open the
windows of Heaven, and pour out floods of grace upon
my soul, but I didn't know how great God was and
how small I was. I talked to the Lord as though it
would take all Heaven to satisfy me, but when the Lord
looked at me it nearly tickled me to death, and he
just touched me and I had to holler, "Hold on a minute." It seemed that God wasted enough grace on me
to save everybody in Texas. Such great billows rolled
over my soul that it seemed that rivers of salvation ran
out of the clouds. It seemed to me that I was a min-

now in the Atlantic ocean. It is beyond the comprehension of man. You just as well try to dip the Atlantic ocean dry with a teaspoon as try to exhaust the resources of God's grace.

We next notice that God has an abundance of life. Our blessed Lord said in John 10: 10: "The thief cometh not but for to steal, and to kill, and destroy; but I am come that they might have life, and that they might have it more abundantly." You see you get life in conversion, and in santification you get the life more abundant. We don't know what we have got when we tell people we are sanctified. It will roll on through the ceaseless ages and will shine, and will get deeper and richer and sweeter. The blessing of sanctification is as deep as the demand of fallen humanity, and is as broad as the compassion of God, and as high as Heaven, and as everlasting as the Rock of Ages, and as sweet as honey, and will fix you up for two worlds.   .

When you get sanctified you actually live in the 36th Psalm. He says in the 7th and 8th verses: "How excellent is thy loving kindness, O God! therefore the children of men put their trust under the shadow of thy wings. They shall be abundantly satisfied with the fatness of thy house; and thou shalt make them drink of the river of thy pleasures." This brings you under the wings of God himself. Could you be in a better place? How much better do you want? Under his wings, in a house of fat things, drinking from a river of pleasure. A river is not a creek, nor is it a spring branch. Just think of a branch widening out and making a creek, and then being turned into a river. Think of a fellow drinking from the Mississippi river and looking for the hole. Why you can't miss it. It don't say that the river is as big as the Mississippi and it don't say that it isn't. I believe it is greater. I believe it is big enough for the whole world to drink from, and it reaches from Adam clear down to Bud. Isn't that wonderful? Get under his wings and into his house of fat things. That don't mean oyster soup and ice cream suppers and strawberry festivals; but where God lives and rules and reigns, and people are filled with the flood of divine love. That's the river of pleasure that abundantly satisfies. That is the blessing which the world is seeking today, but they go to the wrong place for it; they go to the devil's house. Of course, if they get into God's house they must go where God stays. But you talk about your circumstances and say: "If you had these difficulties I have to meet you wouldn't talk about rivers of pleasure and houses of fat things." Well, now my friend, what do you call a circumstance? Do you suppose God ever saw a circumstance or a difficulty? He tells us what he is able to do. But you say it's the place where you live. Oh, no, my friend, it isn't the place you **are** at that makes you shout, but it is the condition you **are** in. It isn't what people say about you that makes you happy, it is what God knows you to be. For we read in the New Testament: "If any man be in Christ Jesus **he** is a new creature. Old things have passed away; be hold, all things are become new." And if all things are new and you walk up the street and meet a fellow and he slaps you on the side of the head, he will get honey all over his hands, and as he licks it off he will get under conviction and come back to see what ailed you; you tell him and he will want the same thing. If your experience has juice in it, it will have teeth, and if it has teeth it will bite, and if it bites of course it will get hold of somebody, and he will holler and when he hollers you will have him located, and then you will know where to work.

Now this leads us up to another step. We read in Jer. 33:6, where he is speaking of the backslidings of the people and the city, and he says: "Behold I will bring it health and cure, and I will cure them, and will reveal unto them the abundance of peace and truth." I suppose peace and truth are the finest ingredients in the Christian life. We read in Isaiah 26:3, "Thou wilt keep him in perfect peace whose mind is stayed on thee because he trusteth in thee." We read again in Psalms 119:165: "Great peace have they that love thy law, and nothing shall offend them." This brings us to the place where the world can't offend us, and we can in everything give thanks. But you say there are some things that you can't be thankful for. If a man were to knock you down with a brick bat, you couldn't thank God for that. Oh, yes, my friend, you could thank God that you didn't knock him down, and that would bring you out ahead. Others say they could not thank God for being lied about. Why yes, my friend, the Book says the liar shall take his part in hell, and not the man that was lied on. And if they lie on you, you have nothing to do but rejoice, for Christ said, "Rejoice and be exceeding glad for great is your reward in Heaven, for so persecuted they the prophets which were before you." Now, Christ says again in John 14:27: "Peace I leave with you; my peace I give unto you; not as the world giveth give I unto you. Let not your heart be troubled, neither let it be afraid." And again we read in Phil. 4:6-7, Paul says: "Be careful for nothing, but in everything by prayer and supplication with thanksgiving let your requests be made known unto God. And the peace of

God which passeth all understanding shall keep your
hearts and minds through Christ Jesus."

There you have got peace located. The understanding is in the head, and peace in the heart, so you see
it passes right by the understanding and hits you in
the heart. But you say that is not the correct render-
ing. Have you got anything that is more correct? The
peace that passes understanding runs right by your
head, and a man's head is nothing but a knot on the end
of his backbone anyway. God is not after your head,
but your heart, which is the seat of your affections.
We would be much better and happier if we would unload our head religion and get something in our hearts.

And now, friend, we have had an abundance of
mercy, an abundance of pardon, an abundance of grace,
an abundance of the Holy Ghost, an abundance of life,
an abundance of satisfaction and an abundance of peace
and truth. And now we bring you to an abundance of
love. We read in Ephesians 3 :14-21 : "For this cause
I bow my knees unto the Father of our Lord Jesus
Christ, of whom the whole family in Heaven and earth
is named, that he would grant you, according to the
riches of his glory, to be strengthened with might by
his Spirit in the inner man; that Christ may dwell
in your hearts by faith; that ye being . rooted and
grounded in love, may be able to comprehend with all

saints what is the breadth and length, and depth and
height; and to know the love of Christ, which passeth
knowledge, that ye might be filled with all the fullness
of God. Now unto him that is able to do exceeding
abundantly above all that we ask or think, according to the power that worketh in us, unto him be glory
in the church by Christ Jesus throughout all ages, world
without end, Amen." Well, of course, he had to say
"amen," there was nothing else to say. He reached the
top and could go no further. He had you filled with
the fullness of God and said he was able to do exceeding abundantly above all we ask or think. We will
never be able to exhaust his love. He takes what nobody else wants, and loves and saves them. His great
loving heart was moved with compassion for me, and
he reached down his loving arms and pulled me up,
and put a song in my mouth and praises in my heart,
and it has been twenty-one years and he has never
thrown up my mean kin-folks to me yet. It makes me
love him and it shows him to be a God of love.

One other thing that brings us to a place where we
are ready for Heaven. Saint Peter writes in Second
Peter, 1:11: "For an entrance shall be ministered
unto you abundantly into the everlasting king.
our Lord and Savior Jesus Christ." So we have
abundant entrance into Heaven. We won't have to hug

the gate post, but with our wedding garment on and all its trimmings we'll go in and run up the streets, probably a mile wide and fifteen hundred miles long, and jump into the river and swim across and climb the tree of life, the fruit of which is as big as your two double fists, and ripens every month in the year. It's without peeling on it or seed in it and so good that it melts in your mouth. I dreamed one night of eating fruit off the tree of life and it was so good that I could hardly eat Texas grub for a week afterwards.

Now, reader, put these graces all together and see if it is not worth while to trust God to supply all your needs. If you have got the thing and live it you will draw. Christ said: "If I be lifted up I will draw all men unto me." I will show you the difference between the people that draw and those who do not. I have had people come to my house and sit down and talk awhile, inquire into the health of the family and the general news and when they would leave they would ask us to come and see them, and we would ask them to come back, and we thought but little of it. There was nothing peculiar about the visit. I have had other people to visit me and somehow when they would come to the door I would find myself going to meet them, bring them in and sit down as near to them as I could get. They also would inquire into our health, talk to us of the goodness of God. Before they would leave they would get down and pray with us and you could feel the presence of the Lord in the home. When they would get up to leave they would walk out into the yard and I would walk right along by them. They would walk out to their buggy and get into it. I would walk up between the hind wheel and the fore wheel and put one foot upon the axle, hold the dashboard and talk as long as they would stay. When they would turn to drive away I would stand and watch them as they would drive off. I'd watch the old buggy till it would get out of sight. I'd walk back into the house and feel a little sad some way and would wonder what ailed me and the light would break in on me that this person had been holding up the Lord and he had been drawing me. Now, friends, you can see the difference between these two visitors. One could draw and the other didn't. The man that draws can fulfill the Scripture where it says: "We are to be all things unto all men that we might win some."

Made in the USA
Middletown, DE
31 October 2022